I0804241

Praise for *The Radical Money Manifesto*:

This book gives a fresh, culturally relevant perspective on stewardship and generosity. Christian generosity is so strategic – God has already given his people more than enough to resource his kingdom.

– **Robert Collins, CFA,** Global Managing Director of TrustBridge Global, formerly with the National Christian Foundation and Goldman Sachs Asset Management

With his background as a church historian and theologian, Dr Black carefully weaves a beautiful tapestry of Scripture, church history, the Church Fathers' teaching, as well as insights of respected contemporary leaders in Africa who give successful church approaches to godly stewardship. His eye-opening explanation of tithing from scriptural and historical perspectives will reset your thinking.

– **Dr Tim Teusink**, teaching medical ethics in Africa with SIM France-Belgium

Dr Black provides us with a timely and very relevant theology of stewardship. He issues a serious call to return to God's mission in all respects. If we let go, we will discover there are resources for what God has called us for. The book is a must read – and a must do!

– **Dr Hannes van der Walt**, Projects Manager for the Association of Christian Religious Practitioners, South Africa

Written by a scholar who was formed and has served both sides – the Global North and Global South, as well as Eastern and the Western Christianity, this is a breath of fresh air when it comes to stewardship and the discipleship it demands.

– **Very Rev Fr Evangelos Thiani (ThD)**, Senior Lecturer at Makarios III Orthodox Patriarchal Seminary, Nairobi-Kenya

With vivid stories, Dr Black outlines a practical approach grounded in the sacrificial example of Jesus Christ to build a lifestyle of stewardship. As a teacher, historian, and seasoned pastor, Dr Black in his own life has "learned the secret of facing plenty and hunger, abundance and want" (Philippians 4:13). This makes his message truly authentic and gives it transformative power.

– **Very Rev Dr John A. Jillions**, author of *Divine Guidance: Lessons for Today from the World of Early Christianity*

Using excellent Kenyan examples, Dr Black reinterprets Christian prosperity within biblical perspective. I recommend it to all Christians who honestly desire to see the church steward the world within God's parameters.

– **Rev Dr Julius Kithinji**, Lecturer and Head of the Department of Theology, Philosophy, and Biblical Studies at St Paul's University, Kenya

You will want to share these lessons with members of your church and Bible study groups!

– **Rev Dr John Michael Kiboi**, Author of *Assurance of Salvation* and Senior Lecturer in the Faculty of Theology at St Paul's University, Kenya

JOSEPH WILLIAM BLACK

THE RADICAL MONEY MANIFESTO

WHAT JESUS TAUGHT AND WE FORGOT

INSIGHT BOOKS
AFRICAN ISSUES
AFRICA'S AUTHORS

OASIS
INTERNATIONAL
PUBLISHING

The Radical Money Manifesto: What Jesus Taught and We Forgot

ISBN 13: 978-1-59452-779-1
ISBN: 1-59452-779-2

Published by Oasis International Ltd.

Oasis International is a ministry devoted to growing discipleship through publishing African voices.

- We *engage* Africa's most influential, most relevant, and best communicators for the sake of the gospel.
- We *cultivate* local and global partnerships in order to publish and distribute high-quality books and Bibles.
- We *create* contextual content that meets the specific needs of Africa, has the power to transform individuals and societies, and gives the church in Africa a global voice.

Oasis is: *Satisfying Africa's Thirst for God's Word*. For more information, go to oasisinternational.com.

Printed in India

21 22 23 24 25 26 27 28 29 30 BPI 10 9 8 7 6 5 4 3 2 1

CONTENTS

The Radical Money Manifesto 7

1: Called to Be Faithful Stewards 11
Bible Study 17

2: Tithing in the Old Testament 19
Bible Study 27

3: Is Tithing for Christians? 33
Bible Study 41

4: Sell All You Have and Give to the Poor 43
Bible Study 49

5: Trust God with Your Financial Future 51
Bible Study 57

6: Sharing All Things in Common 59
Bible Study 67

7: Caring for the Global Body 69
Bible Study 79

8: A Great Cloud of Witnesses: Part One 81
Bible Study 87

9: A Great Cloud of Witnesses: Part Two 91
Bible Study 101

10: Reclaiming Real Stewardship 105
Bible Study 111

About the Author 115
Acknowledgements 117
Endnotes 119

THE RADICAL MONEY MANIFESTO

I need to warn you: what you are about to learn in this book could radically change your life.

You could find yourself with a fresh love for God and a love for others.

Instead of worrying about your finances, you might feel the lightness and freedom that comes from confidence in your Provider God. Instead of envying the rich, you might find yourself generously giving towards the poor. Instead of feeling guilty whenever the word *tithe* is mentioned, you might find a new warmth towards the God who has bestowed all gifts on you.

Does it seem strange that loving God and others more fully would be the result of a book focused on money? Those are the two greatest commandments in the Bible. Shouldn't they be discussed in a book about prayer or evangelism or something that sounds more . . . spiritual?

And yet if you were to admit it, the word *money* might have been what caught your attention in the title. Because money is so important to us.

Too often, money occupies a place in our hearts that should be reserved for God alone. That's why Jesus talked so much about it. He said, "You cannot serve both God and money." That's why a book about money gets to the very heart of our relationship with God and with others. Sometimes, thinking money is not very spiritual is just an excuse not to let God touch that part of our lives. That is exactly when money is blocking us from a fully alive, transformed heart.

We need a radical solution: a new heart. As you will discover in this book, that is precisely what Jesus offers. It is drastic. Jesus calls people to take up their cross – or leave their fishing and tax collecting businesses – to follow him. The call is no less costly today.

And yet it is worth it. What land or bank or stock market offers investment opportunities with eternal payoffs?

This book's message is radical in another sense of the word too. While radical can mean extreme, it can also refer to roots and origins. As we delve into the Bible, we will discover a timeless message. During his ministry, Jesus laid out his manifesto for the Kingdom of God. In his parables and his famous "Sermon on the Mount", he described a bold vision for how we should live in relationship with God and others. He went back to the roots of the Old Testament law and explained God's original intent. It was radical. It sounded extreme. But really, it had been around since the very beginning, when God created humans as stewards.

The early church caught hold of this vision. Their generous community life can seem so shocking to us that we try to make excuses for why we can't live like that today. But when we look at the letters written by the early apostles and the writings of the Church Fathers, we see that they took Jesus's words seriously! These people heard Jesus's radical manifesto. They believed that being a citizen of the Kingdom of Heaven should impact how they responded to the injustice they saw in their churches and cultures. They did zealous things like standing up against corruption or selling their property and giving it to the poor. This was not just one or two people, but examples from centuries of church history.

Could it be instead that we are the ones who have lost our way?

I studied the Bible and church history and taught in seminaries and churches for a decade, frequently wrestling with the true meaning of Christian stewardship with my students. Looking around me, I saw confusion and hurt in our churches about wealth, money, and poverty. In Africa, everyday people miss salaries for months while gambling companies made fortunes. I saw orphanages who could not produce records of how they spent donor funds. I saw churches preach eagerly about one's duty to tithe, but not demonstrate the same enthusiasm to feed the hungry, care for the sick, or visit prisoners. I heard people compare pastors to police officers and politicians, all looking to line their pockets. I realized that in every case, we were not understanding the true teaching of Jesus on stewardship.

That is what motivated me to write a book. I wrote a book for church leaders, *Raising Up Good Stewards*, that tackles problems like dependency and false teachings about wealth and money. It gives practical advice on how church leaders can become more transparent and accountable. And it also delves into the biblical truths you will learn in this book. After I finished, my publisher said that this content was too important to tell only church leaders. Everyone needed to hear it.

The power of this book is not in my own words, but in the words of Jesus. We will encounter the testimony of God's people throughout the Bible and church history. As we do I pray that the Holy Spirit works his miracles of radically changing your heart and attitude about money the way he has done in my own life.

But this book isn't meant for you to read alone. When God gave the command to steward the earth, he gave it to Adam and Eve. When he gave the Old Testament law, it was to the people of Israel. When Jesus called his disciples, he called 12 of them to follow him together. So I encourage you that if you really want to be transformed, read this book with a community.

Find some friends, invite your small group, or ask your pastor if your whole church can read it together. Each chapter has a Bible study guide so that you can engage with the Scriptures yourselves. It has discussion questions for you to deepen your understanding and apply these truths to your lives. As you set aside time to meet in the next 10 sessions, I pray that the living God will work powerfully among you!

I can't wait for you to find out *What Jesus Taught and We Forgot*. I can't wait for you to swap duty for freedom, worry for gratitude, and envy for joy. I can't wait to see you on fire for Jesus, excited about the good news, and overflowing with love for your neighbour because of your new understanding of your calling to steward all God has given us. Shall we begin?

CHAPTER ONE

CALLED TO BE FAITHFUL STEWARDS

All over the world, people care about money – a lot. From sunrise to sunset we hustle to get money and dream about what to do with it. We buy books and attend seminars and watch videos, hoping for answers from successful businesspeople and financial experts.

Unfortunately, our desire for money seems to be creating more problems. Taxpayers' money and donors' aid disappear into corrupt pockets and offshore bank accounts. Bribery affects everyone, down to the traffic police officer and the public transport conductor. Too many people seek leadership positions not to serve people, but to enrich themselves and their friends at everyone else's expense. Our problem may not be a lack of resources as much as a misuse of them.

I wonder if, even in the church, we desire money and a better life but use more spiritual language to express it. We put a little bit in the offering basket to fulfil our duty. We may even give the 10 per cent tithe we believe God commanded in the Old Testament. Perhaps we are convinced that God wants to bless us with prosperity. "If I have enough faith and give to the church," we tell ourselves, "God will move the financial mountains that block my way to the life I deserve."

We seem to believe that more money will solve our problems. Is Christianity about what I can get or what I can give? What has happened to the values of sharing and community that our cultures held? It seems like today we overemphasize the individual, rather than our social responsibility to care for our neighbour.

How much time have we spent considering what Jesus wants us to do with what we have?

Many of us believe we know what the Bible says about money. But how much time have we spent considering what Jesus wants us to do with what we have? It seems we have forgotten that God's first call on us and our congregations is to be good stewards of what he gives us. To discover the radical money manifesto, let's go back to the root of our purpose as human beings.

CREATED TO STEWARD

We human beings were created to care for God's creation. After creating everything else: "God blessed [humans], and God said to them: 'Be fruitful and multiply, and fill the earth and subdue it; and have dominion over the fish of the sea and over the birds of the air and over every living thing that moves upon the earth'" (Genesis 1:28 NRSV-A).

This earth is not ours – God made it. But he gives us the task of watching over and taking care of the creatures and the earth for him (Genesis 1:28; 2:15). God has created us with the job description of managing his creation. As we do this to the glory of God, we reflect his image.

Jesus talked a lot about stewards, especially the difference between good ones and bad ones. In Jesus's day, a steward was a slave whom an estate owner put in charge of managing his affairs. Today, we might picture a man who works in a big city but owns some land in the village. He wants to invest in farming as a side business, while he lives and works in the city. So he hires a farm manager and entrusts him with the resources to oversee the day-to-day needs on the farm. The manager has responsibility over the farm and thus has a powerful position. But he is still a hired worker.

Similarly, the stewards Jesus knew and observed may have had great responsibility for managing property and other slaves, but they were themselves still under the authority of the landowner. Their whole purpose was to serve the master's will.

We were created to be stewards – the farm managers – of God's creation. This is the astonishing message of Genesis 1–2. Everything we have, every shilling or naira or dollar, every relationship and opportunity that comes our way – this is what God gives us to steward.

GREEDY STEWARDS

However, humanity failed to steward God's creation. Genesis 3 tells how Adam and Eve disobeyed God's command not to eat from a tree, and the tragedy that resulted. They were not content with being *made* in God's image. They wanted to be godlike themselves. They misused the authority

God had given them to exercise dominion. When God confronted them, they refused to accept responsibility. Adam blamed Eve, the partner God gave him. She in turn blamed the serpent – ironically, part of the creation she and her husband had been asked to steward. Adam and Eve fell from fellowship with God and with each other.

All humans now share the consequences. Created in the image of God, we are still capable of much that brings God pleasure. But too often we follow the example of our first parents and abuse our authority. God called us to love him, love others, and care for his creation. Instead, we think of ourselves first. We compete with each other, lying, stealing, and killing to plunder creation for our own selfish desires. Our rebellion has bled into the whole fabric of the creation we were intended to manage for God's glory.

RESCUE

But God himself decided to come into our broken world and do something incredible. Jesus came as a human to restore our relationship with God and others. He showed us how to obey God and live unselfishly. He showed us how to forgive each other – even people who hate us. By his death on the cross and his resurrection from the dead, Jesus opens the way for us to experience forgiveness and restoration in all of our relationships, and through us he has begun the process of re-establishing God's kingdom in this world.

Jesus saves us and restores us to who we were created to be. We were made to love God with all our heart and to love our neighbour as ourselves. When we know God loves us, we can love each other. When we repent for our sin, God begins to change our selfish hearts. Salvation reconciles us with God and the people around us.

God invites us to join him in his mission to restore the world.

Jesus also calls us to reclaim our original job description as stewards of God's creation. Salvation means living out our original purpose to use God's gifts for his glory. He invites us to join him in his mission to restore the world, becoming part of God's kingdom right here and right now. We begin to sacrifice our resources, our time, and our abilities to God to use for his glory.

Here is an example: Jane came from a small village, but she was a gifted student and worked hard. She dreamed of becoming a doctor to help people. After completing medical school and all her training in her country, many of her classmates left for Europe or America where they could make a lot of money. But Jane felt God had called her to serve in the rural areas she had come from. Her friends thought she had lost her mind. But she knew God had given her all her training and opportunities. She was determined to be a good steward of it and bless others.

A NEW CREATION

A Swahili saying recently caught my attention: "To run is not necessarily to arrive." Many people are very busy, busy trying to succeed, busy being religious. But given all the effort, one wonders why so little change happens around us and in our own lives. But God's purposes never change. What God values remains as true today as it was yesterday. His goals are clear and have been clear from the beginning. God's goal is to restore his original plan – that his creation would glorify him and that the people he created in his image would steward his creation.

God's people, whom God is saving, become the means of God's grace for those around us. We are the beachhead for the invasion of God's kingdom on this planet. How we respond to God's love to us in Christ will be mirrored by both our response to our neighbour and the creation around us. It calls us to embrace our part in God's big story about stewardship:

Creation: Stewardship is what God made us for.

Fall: Almost every destructive problem we face stems from abandoning our calling to steward.

Rescue: Through Jesus, God saves his world and restores us to the stewards we were meant to be.

New Creation: Our eternal calling is to be stewards in God's kingdom.

Eventually, God will fully save us from the destruction and death caused by our rebellion. Like God intended in the Garden of Eden, he will live with his people, and "death will be no more; mourning and crying and pain will be no more" (Revelation 21:1-5).

God will "create new heavens and a new earth" and bring us back to life there (Isaiah 65:17). Creation will be restored so that even animals will be at peace with each other (Isaiah 65:25).

Just as stewardship was our job description in the Garden of Eden, stewardship will be our job description in the New Jerusalem. God's chosen people will build houses, plant vineyards, and "shall long enjoy the work of their hands" (Isaiah 65:17-23). We will live forever as image-bearers of God. God will make all things new in Christ, resurrecting and restoring his creation.

Although this will not fully be a reality until Jesus returns, in the meantime God calls us not just to come to him, but also to be stewards in this place. As we do, we become part of God's answer, God's means for saving his world. What could be more important?

God is breaking into human history right now, to reclaim this place and these lives for his kingdom. In individuals and communities, God is raising up stewards who reflect his image and proclaim his glory. These give us hope that it is possible to be better stewards of what God has given us.

A TANZANIAN STEWARD

One of these new stewards is a friend of mine who distributed veterinary supplies to retail shops in rural Tanzania. He met corruption at every step: importers, government inspectors, wholesalers, and local vendors. He had to pay so much under-the-counter money that it seemed impossible to stay in business. He grew angry at the corrupt system.

He offered himself to God to use however he chose.

Then he heard a simple sermon. It was not about how to get the success you want from God. Instead he heard that God was setting him free, giving him the power to live for God, and freeing him to love others. He began to view himself as the Lord's, and that all he had was now the Lord's. In response to God's goodness, he realized he needed to hand everything over to God, including his business. He offered himself to God to use however he chose.

My friend began to talk with his suppliers about the bribes they requested. Some were angry and defensive. But others were bothered about the web of corruption that had trapped them all. They began to find ways to avoid the bribes and kickbacks that characterized so much of the business. Even with those who maintained the old ways of doing business, my friend developed a reputation for honesty.

Because he no longer paid bribes, he passed on the savings to his clients, which they often passed on to their customers. He also rethought how to use his income. Before he became a Christian, he had avoided religious giving because he didn't trust those who handled the money. But now he noticed that he had the means to meet serious needs around him. He intervened in that widow's life, this orphanage, that church's feeding programme, that girl's tuition.

He did not draw attention to himself, but he made a difference in a growing circle of people. He became known as a generous man. The more he gave, the more he seemed to have. His family always had enough. He became a real disciple, living out what Jesus told his disciples when he sent them out to preach: "Freely you have received, freely give" (Matthew 10:8 NIV).

As my salesman friend found, Jesus has a radical agenda for our money that can transform every part of our lives. In each chapter and the accompanying Bible study questions, we will dive into the Bible's call to be good stewards. It came from the Old Testament. It revolutionized the early church. Church Fathers boldly lived it out in their communities. As you hear these inspiring stories and challenging truths, my prayer is that you hear Jesus call you to trust him with all you are and all you have.

If you do, I know you, too, can experience the joy and blessing of stewardship. You can learn how to live out God's call for you. You can become what you were created to be. But be warned. This book will revolutionize the way you look at what you have and what you choose to do with it. It will challenge you to listen to what the Bible says about resources in a new way. If you will dare to take up the challenge, your finances, work, and relationship with God might never be the same.

BIBLE STUDY ONE

CALLED TO BE FAITHFUL STEWARDS

Stewardship isn't a concept churches invented to raise money, nor is it simply setting aside money for the offering. When we start exploring what the Bible has to say, we discover that stewardship is much more foundational. We human beings are not here by accident. God made us for a reason. From the very beginning, being a steward has been a significant part of our purpose and what it means to be made in God's image. Stewardship is our first job description!

After God created the rest of creation, humans were created in God's own image and immediately appointed as stewards. Let's read about our original calling to stewardship in Genesis 1:26-31. Scripture quotations are taken from the New Revised Standard Version, Anglicised.

Genesis 1:26-31

26 Then God said, 'Let us make humankind in our image, according to our likeness; and let them have dominion over the fish of the sea, and over the birds of the air, and over the cattle, and over all the wild animals of the earth, and over every creeping thing that creeps upon the earth.'

27 So God created humankind in his image,
in the image of God he created them;
male and female he created them.

28 God blessed them, and God said to them, 'Be fruitful and multiply, and fill the earth and subdue it; and have dominion over the fish of the sea and over the birds of the air and over every living thing that
moves upon the earth.' 29 God said, 'See, I have given you every plant yielding seed that is upon the face of all the earth, and every tree with
seed in its fruit; you shall have them for food. 30 And to every beast of the earth, and to every bird of the air, and to everything that creeps on

the earth, everything that has the breath of life, I have given every green plant for food.' And it was so. [31] God saw everything that he had made, and indeed, it was very good. And there was evening and there was morning, the sixth day.

Questions to Discuss

1. When God tells the humans to govern and reign, their only example of someone who governs and reigns would have been God. Describe how God governs his creation and reigns over the things that he has made.
2. Humans are made in the image of God and given this calling to rule and govern. Which aspects of God's way of governing that we just described would apply to us?
3. Can you give some contemporary examples of where we have done what God created us to do? Can you give some examples of how we have missed the mark in our calling as stewards today?
4. Jesus restores our relationships with God, one another, and creation. What are some specific and practical ways that knowing Jesus changes our stewardship?
5. In your church or Christian community, to what extent do you see people linking their faith and their finances? What impact does this have on your relationships within the church and your witness to the surrounding community?
6. Discuss as a group what your expectations are of each other as you read this book together. For instance, when and where will you meet? What should you prepare before you meet? How will you respect each other in conversation? Pray expectantly for God's Spirit to speak and work within you as you study his Word.

CHAPTER TWO

TITHING IN THE OLD TESTAMENT

In this book, we will study what the Bible says and what the early church practised when it came to money, stewardship, and giving. We'll begin with a look at tithing, a way many Christians are told to manage their money, which comes from the Old Testament. It is appealing because it seems so simple and so *biblical*. But is tithing the answer, especially when we look more closely at what the Scriptures actually say?

Churches all over the world encourage their members to tithe. For pastors and elder boards, tithing is an easy concept to grasp and communicate. Could it be any clearer than an obligation to give "10 per cent for the Lord"? No doubt the concept is easier for you and me to understand than to practise, if the money we make barely covers rent, food, school fees, transport, and helping with extended family needs.

But then, like most African Christians, we also have many preachers' favourite tithing passage ringing in our ears:

> Will anyone rob God? Yet you are robbing me! But you say, "How are we robbing you?" In your tithes and offerings! You are cursed with a curse, for you are robbing me – the whole nation of you! Bring the full tithe into the storehouse, so that there may be food in my house, and thus put me to the test, says the Lord of hosts; see if I will not open the windows of heaven for you and pour down for you an overflowing blessing (Malachi 3:8-10 NRSV-A).

When you hear this reminder from your church leaders, perhaps you feel guilty. You do not want to disappoint God, much less call down a curse on your head and on your nation! So maybe you give whenever you hear this message, but you still struggle to manage 10 per cent consistently.

On the other hand, perhaps this Scripture excites you with hope. You imagine that all your other money problems will be solved by the promise that God will pour down his overflowing blessing! Maybe you give in faith, trusting that God will provide for your needs. Perhaps you or someone around you has a testimony of how God has provided for you because you decided to trust him and tithe.

Your church may be struggling with finances. Perhaps the church leadership expects the pastor to work full time at church, but there is not enough offering for both the needs of the church and the pastor's family. So, the pastor or the pastor's spouse must find another way of supplementing the family income.

Perhaps tithing seems like an easy solution. If all the people in the church gave 10 per cent, the result would be that as soon as there were 10 employed people in the church the pastor would have the average of their income each month. Of course, there should be more church members than that, so that the church's needs would be sorted out and the church would have extra funds for ministering to the community, hosting visitors, and building better facilities.

WHAT DOES THE BIBLE ACTUALLY SAY?

The financial needs of the church in Africa and its members are real. But as we look at the actual biblical evidence, we discover that the Old Testament concept of tithing may not be the answer for New Testament stewards like us. So where does the idea of tithing come from?

It comes from verses found throughout the Old Testament, in the law God gave the people of Israel. Before we treat the Old Testament as if it directly applies to us today, we need to ask why it was written and for what purpose. We should not treat this ancient collection of stories, poems, histories, and prophecies as God's direct word for whatever situation we face. I am not saying that the Old Testament is irrelevant to us today. It certainly has God-given value. We just need to maintain the big picture.

A principle of good Bible interpretation is that we must understand the books of the Bible as they were originally intended before we apply them to our lives.

The various books that make up the Old Testament were written to the nation of Israel. A principle of good Bible interpretation is that we must understand them as they were originally intended before we apply them to our lives. To unlock the unified message of the Old Testament in general, and commands like tithing in particular, we must understand that the commands were given in the context of a specific agreement that God made with Israel, also called a *covenant* (Exodus 19–24). Once we grasp what God is doing with his covenant with Israel, we will understand the Old Testament as we never have before.

GOD'S COVENANT WITH ISRAEL[1]

In ancient Near Eastern history, a covenant was an agreement made between two parties – often between a greater king and a lesser conquered people. The king usually identified himself on the basis of the great feats he had accomplished, and for his part, agreed to protect the newly conquered people and provide necessary services. The people agreed to keep the king's laws, pay taxes, and provide a certain number of young men, horses, and supplies for his army. Then the gods would be called to bless the people for keeping the covenant or curse them if they broke it and rebelled against their lord. There would usually be a long list of terrible things that the king would threaten to do to the people should they throw off the yoke of his reign over them. These are the types of covenants that were common among Israel's neighbours in the time of Genesis and Exodus.

The covenant we find in Exodus, Leviticus, Numbers, and Deuteronomy is similar to this. The great king *Yahweh* (God's Hebrew name is unpronounceable, so it is always translated in English as the Lord or Lord) identified himself as the one who saved Israel from Egypt with mighty acts of power. He called Israel to be his people and promised that he would be their God. "I am the Lord your God, who brought you out of the land of Egypt, out of the house of slavery" (Exodus 20:2). Then he outlined the conditions of the covenant – the laws about how his people will relate to him and to one another. These were summarized in the Ten Commandments (Exodus 20:3-17) and expanded through the rest of the *Torah* (the name in Hebrew given to the first five books of the Hebrew Scriptures).

God's covenantal commands covered almost every aspect of Israel's life and worship. Not only were there commands about what sacrifices to bring, when to bring them, and how to offer them, but there were commands about the various festivals to be held every year. God commanded the Israelites to refrain from working every seventh day (the Sabbath). He commanded them to eat only certain kinds of animals and not others. He commanded ritual purification after contact with a dead body or sexual relations – emissions (for men) and menstruation (for women). God commanded mothers to be purified after childbirth and baby boys to be circumcised. Also as part of God's covenant commandments, God required each family to bring their tithes and offerings to the Lord. These were all part of the covenant that God made with Israel at Mount Sinai.

Along with the covenant's obligations, God also promised benefits or blessings for faithfulness and obedience. There were also stern warnings about what would happen if the people chose to rebel and follow other gods or if they did not keep God's commandments.

Covenants like this one would then be ratified with all the people participating in solemn sacrifices. They would agree to fulfil all that the king required of them, and the king would agree to do all that he had promised to do for them.

ISRAEL FAILED TO KEEP THE COVENANT[2]

Tragically, Israel chose again and again to rebel against Yahweh. They broke the covenant, calling down on their heads the curses God declared would happen if his people ever left him for other gods or otherwise broke the relationship between them. The historical books of the Old Testament tell how again and again the people went their own way, experienced terrible judgement, and then came back to the Lord in repentance.

God was extremely long-suffering; he did not give up on his people. He sent a new type of character, the prophet, who called the people of Israel to account and warned them of God's coming judgement if they did not repent. Let me point out that the prophets of the Bible do not exactly match our cultural understanding of prophets. Many African cultures see a prophet as a holy man who can foretell the future, who mediates between factions in the community, and who presides at sacrifices or other religious functions. Old Testament prophets such as Samuel, for example, sometimes filled these roles in the community. But the main reason God raised up prophets was to remind his people of the covenant they had solemnly made with him and to warn them of being cursed by the threatened judgement if they persisted in their rebellion.

We might say that Old Testament prophets were God's lawyers.

We might say that Old Testament prophets were God's lawyers, making a case against God's people who had broken their covenant agreement and the law. Their writings are full of both the threats of judgement for having left their God and also the promise of God's blessing if they repent and come back "home". To give a clear example, listen again to the words of the prophet Malachi quoted earlier:

> Will anyone rob God? Yet you are robbing me! But you say, "How are we robbing you?" In your tithes and offerings! You are cursed with a curse, for you are robbing me – the whole nation of you! Bring the full tithe into the storehouse, so that there may be food in my house, and thus put me to the test, says the Lord of hosts; see if I will not open the windows of heaven for you and pour down for you an overflowing blessing (Malachi 3:8-10).

Now that we know the story of the Old Testament, the covenant, and the role of a prophet, this Scripture makes more sense. Malachi was reminding Israel that they had made a covenant with the Lord, promising to tithe. They would be cursed if they broke the covenant and abundantly blessed if they were faithful to the covenant. All of these curses and blessings were based on the fact that Israel and the Lord had made a covenant long before, in the time of Moses.

Unfortunately, even after all the prophets' warnings, Israel still failed to keep God's covenant. So, God brought about the judgement he had promised. The 10 northern tribes of Israel were defeated and scattered all over the Middle East by the Assyrians. Not long afterwards, the Kingdom of Judah was crushed by the Babylonians. Jerusalem was destroyed, the Temple was burned, and the survivors were taken in captivity to Babylon. And even after the exiles returned, they still struggled to take God's covenant seriously. This is the context of Malachi's prophecy – a warning to take their covenantal relationship with God seriously, or even worse things would befall them. Judea continued on, but mostly as a small province constantly pressured by the surrounding peoples to abandon their covenant and conform to their neighbours' ways of living. Except for a brief period before the Romans, they never fully recovered as a people, but lived under constant threat of annihilation by their more powerful neighbours. The New Testament begins with the Jewish people suffering under Roman rule, hoping that God will come to their aid and deliver them from their enemies.

TITHING IN THE OLD COVENANT

As we have seen, tithing was one of the conditions, or commandments, that God gave to Israel as part of his covenant with them. The purpose for these tithes was to support Israel's worship as well as provide for the poor. But there has been a lot of confusion, not just about who is obligated to pay these tithes, but even how much a tithe was in Israel's day.

Most of our churches teach that the Old Testament tithe is 10 per cent of one's income, so we should give 10 per cent to our churches. Some churches even make giving 10 per cent a requirement for membership. But is this 10 per cent figure what we find in God's law? It will likely come as a shock, but nowhere does the Old Testament teach or require that members of the Sinai covenant community are meant to give only 10 per cent. I believe when we study the laws of the Old Testament, we see that the required figure is actually significantly *more.*

Here's how Moses put it in Deuteronomy 12:5-19, 14:22-26, and 26:1-15. Every head of household was required to give 10 per cent for the support and upkeep of the Tabernacle/Temple and to provide for the Levites, who had no land inheritance. Then, every head of household was required to contribute a *second* 10 per cent of their income, intended to cover expenses when the family travelled to Jerusalem for the major festivals every year. Finally, a *third* 10 per cent was to be collected every three years (for an average of 3.3 per cent per year) for the widows, orphans, and refugees in one's local area.

The Old Testament tithe *is not 10 per cent, it's actually 23.3 per cent of one's income every year?*

Does it surprise you to learn that the Old Testament tithe *is not 10 per cent, it's actually 23.3 per cent of one's income every year?* The modern concept of tithing just 10 per cent to the church, which is so prevalent in many of our churches, is thus actually less than the Old Testament concept.

Now, I'm not suggesting the formula for pleasing God is to give 23.3

per cent of your income to church. That commandment to tithe was given in the context of the covenant God made with his people Israel at Mount Sinai – the same as circumcision, keeping the Sabbath, and kosher eating restrictions. This system was intended for the nation of Israel, not for any of Israel's neighbouring people.[3] God made this covenant with Israel – not with any other nation nor with the non-Jewish Christians who came along 1200 years later.

This raises the question: are we Christians today Israel? Are Christians obliged to keep the commands of the Old Covenant like tithing, eating certain foods, and having a central place of worship for the whole nation? We will return to this question in the next chapter and its Bible study. For now, I just want to highlight that much of what we think we know about tithing isn't really what the Bible is saying.

BIBLE STUDY TWO

TITHING IN THE OLD TESTAMENT

Tithing played an important role in Israel's relationship with God in the Old Testament. Giving a portion of one's harvest or income was one of the conditions that God gave to Israel as part of his covenant with them. These tithes helped to support Israel's worship as well as provide for those who did not have land. But there has been a lot of confusion about who is obligated to pay these tithes and how much a tithe was in Israel's day. Let's gain some clarity by looking at the Scriptures in the Old Testament law for ourselves.

Israel was promised God's blessings if they kept his covenant, and they were threatened with God's curses if they broke his covenant. The story of this covenant and the details of the law are presented in Exodus and Numbers. Deuteronomy is the record of the renewal of God's covenant with Israel. These books include a number of references to giving a tenth, or a tithe. As you read each of the following passages, note down how many different tithes are mentioned and the purposes of each one.

Numbers 18:20-29

> 20 Then the Lord said to Aaron: You shall have no allotment in their
> land, nor shall you have any share among them; I am your share and
> your possession among the Israelites.
>
> 21 To the Levites I have given every tithe in Israel for a possession in
> return for the service that they perform, the service in the tent of
> meeting. 22 From now on the Israelites shall no longer approach the
> tent of meeting, or else they will incur guilt and die. 23 But the Levites
> shall perform the service of the tent of meeting, and they shall bear
> responsibility for their own offences; it shall be a perpetual statute
> throughout your generations. But among the Israelites they shall have

no allotment, 24 because I have given to the Levites as their portion the
tithe of the Israelites, which they set apart as an offering to the Lord.
Therefore I have said of them that they shall have no allotment among
the Israelites.

25 Then the Lord spoke to Moses, saying: 26 You shall speak to the
Levites, saying: When you receive from the Israelites the tithe that I
have given you from them for your portion, you shall set apart an
offering from it to the Lord, a tithe of the tithe. 27 It shall be reckoned
to you as your gift, the same as the grain of the threshing-floor and
the fullness of the wine press. 28 Thus you also shall set apart an
offering to the Lord from all the tithes that you receive from the
Israelites; and from them you shall give the Lord's offering to the priest
Aaron. 29 Out of all the gifts to you, you shall set apart every offering
due to the Lord; the best of all of them is the part to be consecrated.

Deuteronomy 12:5-19

5 But you shall seek the place that the Lord your God will choose out of
all your tribes as his habitation to put his name there. You shall go
there, 6 bringing there your burnt-offerings and your sacrifices, your
tithes and your donations, your votive gifts, your freewill-offerings,
and the firstlings of your herds and flocks. 7 And you shall eat there in
the presence of the Lord your God, you and your households together,
rejoicing in all the undertakings in which the Lord your God has
blessed you.

8 You shall not act as we are acting here today, all of us according to
our own desires, 9 for you have not yet come into the rest and the
possession that the Lord your God is giving you. 10 When you cross
over the Jordan and live in the land that the Lord your God is allotting
to you, and when he gives you rest from your enemies all around so
that you live in safety, 11 then you shall bring everything that I
command you to the place that the Lord your God will choose as a
dwelling for his name: your burnt-offerings and your sacrifices, your
tithes and your donations, and all your choice votive gifts that you
vow to the Lord. 12 And you shall rejoice before the Lord your God, you
together with your sons and your daughters, your male and female

slaves, and the Levites who reside in your towns (since they have no
allotment or inheritance with you).

13 Take care that you do not offer your burnt-offerings at any place you
happen to see. 14 But only at the place that the Lord will choose in one
of your tribes—there you shall offer your burnt-offerings and there
you shall do everything I command you.

15 Yet whenever you desire you may slaughter and eat meat within
any of your towns, according to the blessing that the Lord your God
has given you; the unclean and the clean may eat of it, as they would
of gazelle or deer. 16 The blood, however, you must not eat; you shall
pour it out on the ground like water. 17 Nor may you eat within your
towns the tithe of your grain, your wine, or your oil, the firstlings of
your herds or your flocks, any of your votive gifts that you vow, your
freewill-offerings, or your donations; 18 these you shall eat in the
presence of the Lord your God at the place that the Lord your God
will choose, you together with your son and your daughter, your
male and female slaves, and the Levites resident in your towns,
rejoicing in the presence of the Lord your God in all your undertakings.
19 Take care that you do not neglect the Levite as long as you live in
your land.

Deuteronomy 14:22-29

22 Set apart a tithe of all the yield of your seed that is brought in yearly
from the field. 23 In the presence of the LORD your God, in the place that
he will choose as a dwelling for his name, you shall eat the tithe of
your grain, your wine, and your oil, as well as the firstlings of your herd
and flock, so that you may learn to fear the LORD your God always.
24 But if, when the LORD your God has blessed you, the distance is so
great that you are unable to transport it, because the place where the
LORD your God will choose to set his name is too far away from you,
25 then you may turn it into money. With the money secure in hand, go
to the place that the LORD your God will choose; 26 spend the money for
whatever you wish—oxen, sheep, wine, strong drink, or whatever you
desire. And you shall eat there in the presence of the LORD your God,
you and your household rejoicing together. 27 As for the Levites

resident in your towns, do not neglect them, because they have no
allotment or inheritance with you.

[28] Every third year you shall bring out the full tithe of your produce for
that year, and store it within your towns; [29] the Levites, because they
have no allotment or inheritance with you, as well as the resident
aliens, the orphans, and the widows in your towns, may come and eat
their fill so that the LORD your God may bless you in all the work that
you undertake.

Deuteronomy 26:1-15

[1] When you have come into the land that the Lord your God is giving
you as an inheritance to possess, and you possess it, and settle in it,
[2] you shall take some of the first of all the fruit of the ground, which
you harvest from the land that the Lord your God is giving you, and
you shall put it in a basket and go to the place that the Lord your God
will choose as a dwelling for his name. [3] You shall go to the priest who
is in office at that time, and say to him, 'Today I declare to the Lord
your God that I have come into the land that the Lord swore to our
ancestors to give us.' [4] When the priest takes the basket from your
hand and sets it down before the altar of the Lord your God, [5] you shall
make this response before the Lord your God: 'A wandering Aramean
was my ancestor; he went down into Egypt and lived there as an alien,
few in number, and there he became a great nation, mighty and
populous. [6] When the Egyptians treated us harshly and afflicted us, by
imposing hard labour on us, [7] we cried to the Lord, the God of our
ancestors; the Lord heard our voice and saw our affliction, our toil, and
our oppression. [8] The Lord brought us out of Egypt with a mighty
hand and an outstretched arm, with a terrifying display of power, and
with signs and wonders; [9] and he brought us into this place and gave
us this land, a land flowing with milk and honey. [10] So now I bring the
first of the fruit of the ground that you, O Lord, have given me.' You
shall set it down before the Lord your God and bow down before the
Lord your God. [11] Then you, together with the Levites and the aliens
who reside among you, shall celebrate with all the bounty that the
Lord your God has given to you and to your house.

[12] When you have finished paying all the tithe of your produce in the
third year (which is the year of the tithe), giving it to the Levites, the
aliens, the orphans, and the widows, so that they may eat their fill
within your towns, [13] then you shall say before the Lord your God: 'I
have removed the sacred portion from the house, and I have given it to
the Levites, the resident aliens, the orphans, and the widows, in
accordance with your entire commandment that you commanded me;
I have neither transgressed nor forgotten any of your commandments:
[14] I have not eaten of it while in mourning; I have not removed any of it
while I was unclean; and I have not offered any of it to the dead. I have
obeyed the Lord my God, doing just as you commanded me. [15] Look
down from your holy habitation, from heaven, and bless your people
Israel and the ground that you have given us, as you swore to our
ancestors—a land flowing with milk and honey.'

Questions to Discuss

1. As you read the passages above, how many different tithes did you note down were mentioned? What was the purpose of each one?
2. Can you remember your first exposure to the concept of tithing? What have you been taught about it in Christian walk or at your church?
3. How does this compare with what you have previously thought about the number of tithes and the purpose of tithing?
4. When you read the biblical explanations of the various ways God intended Israel to use the tithes, what do you learn about God's priorities and concerns for using resources?
5. Share with the group one question you have about God's view of finances that you hope to find an answer to during this study.

CHAPTER THREE

IS TITHING FOR CHRISTIANS?

As we discovered in the last chapter, tithing played an important role in Israel's covenant relationship with God in the Old Testament. Each household gave one tenth of their produce to support worship and the Levites. They spent another tenth of their income on celebrating annual religious festivals in Jerusalem. Every three years, families gave yet another a tenth of their income to support local widows, orphans, and refugees.

Today, our circumstances look a bit different. How are we Christians supposed to interpret and apply the Old Testament? Even if we can't articulate why, many of us sense a difference between the Old Testament and the New Testament. For instance, we don't stone idolaters nor do we tear down houses where mildew has been discovered. Something has changed so that we don't feel many of these Old Testament passages are binding on Christians today. What is it that makes Christians still feel that they are being faithful to the Scriptures even if they are not keeping the commandments found in the law given to Israel?

As we try to understand how we should interpret the commandment to tithe as Christians, we find ourselves asking a bigger question: How do we apply the Bible's many other commands about sacrificing, eating kosher, keeping Sabbath, and circumcising baby boys? It was written for the children of Israel, but what does it mean for the rest of us who are not Jews?[4]

Christians have struggled with this from the earliest days of the church until now. In fact, Acts records a massive conflict on this very issue. Plenty of Christians in Jerusalem were convinced that Christianity was essentially an add-on component to their Judaism. When Gentiles began becoming Christians through the ministries of Peter, Philip, Paul, and Barnabas, many Jewish Christians were scandalized. They struggled to believe that non-Jews could become Christians. So, they insisted that all Christians, both Jews and Gentiles, keep the Old Testament covenant. This meant that a Gentile man would have to get circumcised in order to be a real

Christian, as well as eat kosher, keep the Sabbath, and follow all the other Old Testament laws.

This understanding of Christianity was very different from the one the apostles had been preaching. The issue was so serious that Paul and other apostles in Jerusalem felt that the gospel itself was being threatened. The church's leadership needed to decide how Christians would relate to the Jewish Scriptures and its covenant commands. They had to discern: Is the Jesus movement just a sect within Judaism, or is Jesus doing something bigger, something more universal?

It was so important to get this right that they called a special conference of leaders in Jerusalem (see Acts 15). James, the overseer, or bishop of the Jerusalem church, presided. They heard from all of the people involved. They heard the opinion of Jewish Christians. They heard from the apostles Paul and Barnabas, who argued that even Jews couldn't fully keep the Jewish covenant, so Jesus had come both to save Jews from the curse of their failure and to make a way for Gentiles to be saved apart from the Jewish law. It was a complicated argument, but for the sake of the gospel they worked through it. They came to a resolution that saved the church from division and saved the gospel from being obliterated.

Christianity was not Judaism.

These first Christians made a very important decision that day. It had implications for the subsequent history of the church right up to our present day. They decided that *Christianity was not Judaism.* In other words, the Jewish Scriptures were not written directly for Christians in the same way they were for Jews. God did not make his covenant at Mount Sinai with Gentiles or with Christians; he made his covenant with Jews. The prophets were usually not addressing Gentiles, much less Christians; they were calling Jews to repent for breaking their covenant with God. So, the rules, regulations, and obligations we find in the Old Testament were intended for the Jews and Jews alone – not for Gentiles.[5]

Paul, Peter, James, and the first Christians understood that the primary blessing from the Hebrew Scriptures is that we learn about God and his ways, and of his promises to send a Saviour. The Sinai covenant did not apply to Gentiles, but the Jewish Scriptures still revealed many relevant things about the power, character, and plans of God. The Scriptures also pointed to a future salvation that God would accomplish when he sent a Saviour. The Messiah would deliver his people from their rebellion against God and the curses that such rebellion brought upon their lives and their nation. These same Scriptures also explained that God was not finished with the many nations across the world. His Messiah would open the way for his blessing to come to them as well.

When Jesus came as the Messiah, he did what Israel never could; he kept both the letter and the spirit of God's law. Israel, just like the rest of humanity, had rebelled against God, become alienated from God, and become lost to sin and death. Jesus saves Israel from the covenant curses that destroyed Israel when they left the way of the Torah, and Jesus saves us from the curses of our own estrangement from God and from our resulting death by taking the consequences of our fall upon himself. His death on the cross ratified a *new* covenant open to all people, which we celebrate in the Eucharist. This New Covenant would be about repentance, relationship, and forgiveness, not the commandments, condemnation, and curses of the old.

Jesus defeated the power of sin and death and rose again from the dead. He is the beginning of God's new creation and new humanity. By the power of the Holy Spirit, when we resurrect from the dead on the Last Day, we will become part of that new humanity. As Jeremiah prophesied: "'This is the covenant that I will make with the house of Israel after those days,' says the Lord. 'I will put my law within them, and I will write it on their hearts; and I will be their God, and they shall be my people'" (Jeremiah 31:33 NRSV-A). Ezekiel declares: "A new heart I will give you, and a new spirit I will put within you; and I will remove from your body the heart of stone and give you a heart of flesh" (Ezekiel 36:26).

Because of Jesus, *all* nations are invited to become part of the New Covenant community, whose mission is to establish New Covenant communities of Jesus-followers to the ends of the earth.

THE BIG ISSUE FOR PAUL

Even after the Jerusalem Council's decision, some early Christians assumed that they were still obligated to keep the Old Testament commands. Like many of us today, they had a very difficult time understanding the new regimen for followers of Jesus. But Paul insisted that as Christians under the New Covenant, it is crucial that we do not put ourselves back under the Jewish Torah.

Paul makes this point forcefully in his letter to the churches in Galatia. He was upset to discover that Jewish Christians had been following him from town to town during his recent mission there, seeking to persuade the Galatian Christians to abandon Paul's gospel. These troublemakers taught that for people's Christianity to be viable they must embrace and keep the Jewish covenant in order to become true members of God's special people.

This is not a matter of different interpretations; the gospel itself is in danger.

Paul was furious. You can still feel the heat of his anger when he writes: "I am astonished that you are so quickly deserting the one who called you in the grace of Christ and are turning to a different gospel – not that there is another gospel, but there are some that are confusing you and want to pervert the gospel of Christ" (Galatians 1:6-7). Notice that for Paul, this is not a matter of different interpretations; the gospel itself is in danger. The threat introduced by these false teachers is so real that Paul declares: "But even if we or an angel from heaven should proclaim to you a gospel contrary to what we proclaimed to you, let that one be accursed!" (Galatians 1:8). These are very strong words.

Paul was so convicted that it was wrong to go back to living under the Torah that at one point he directly confronted Peter about this very issue. In another part of his letter to the Galatians, he describes how Peter struggled to be consistent in his understanding about the gospel and whether Christians should continue to live like Jews under the Old Covenant or not. So, we are not alone in finding it difficult to separate ourselves from the Old Testament law.

In Antioch, which had been Paul and Barnabas's home base for their missionary journeys, Jewish and Gentile Christians mixed freely and had fellowship together. This was against Jewish law, which said Jews could not associate with or eat with Gentiles. During a visit, Peter had been freely eating with all the Christians in Antioch. But when he heard that some of the Jewish Christians that demanded Gentile circumcision were arriving from Jerusalem he separated himself from the Gentile believers and stayed with the Jewish believers.

Paul felt that this was more than just hypocrisy: " 'If you, though a Jew, live like a Gentile and not like a Jew, how can you compel the Gentiles to live like Jews?' We ourselves are Jews by birth and not Gentile sinners; yet we know that a person is justified not by the works of the law but through faith in Jesus Christ" (Galatians 2:14b-16a).

I need to add here an important point that is not clear in English. In Galatians, every time the apostle Paul uses the word translated into English as "law", he is using the Greek translation of the Hebrew word *Torah*. This word means "instruction", but it also stands for the first five books of the Hebrew Scriptures and thus for the Sinai covenant contained therein. The issue for Paul is not keeping generic laws or doing good works to be saved. Rather, Paul is saying something that would be shocking for a Jew to say: Jews are not saved by keeping *Torah,* and by their resulting identity as Jews. "We have come to believe in Christ Jesus, so that we might be justified by faith in Christ, and not by doing the works of the law [*Torah]* because no one will be justified by the works of the law [*Torah*]" (Galatians 2:16). These "works of the law [*Torah*]" are none other than those things which set Jews apart from the rest of the Gentile world, which included circumcision, eating kosher, keeping the Sabbath, and tithing.

Paul is clearly vexed:

> You foolish Galatians! Who has bewitched you? . . . The only thing I want to learn from you is this: Did you receive the Spirit by doing the works of the law [*Torah*] or by believing what you heard? Are you so foolish? Having started with the Spirit, are you now ending with the flesh? (Galatians 3:1-3).

Then Paul cuts to the heart of his issue with the Galatians. He says we are not justified by following the *Torah* as Christians, for the simple reason that:

> All who rely on the works of the law [*Torah*] are under a curse; for it is written "Cursed is everyone who does not observe and obey all the things written in the book of the law [*Torah*]." Now it is evident that no

one is justified before God by the law [*Torah*]; for 'The one who is righteous will live by faith.' . . . Christ redeemed us from the curse of the law [*Torah*] by becoming a curse for us – for it is written, "Cursed is everyone who hangs on a tree" – in order that in Christ Jesus the blessing of Abraham might come to the Gentiles, so that we might receive the promise of the Spirit through faith (Galatians 3:10-14).

The implications of Paul's argument are clear and startling. When we Christians force ourselves and others to keep the Old Testament laws, we try to do something that even the Jews couldn't do. Paul's point is that the Jews have reaped again and again the curses that come upon those who cannot and will not keep the stipulations of the Sinai covenant. He cannot imagine that anyone would be so insane as to want to go back into an arrangement that leads only to destruction. Paul could not be more adamant:

> Listen! I, Paul, am telling you that if you let yourselves be circumcised, Christ will be of no benefit to you. Once again, I testify to every man who lets himself be circumcised that he is obliged to obey the entire law [*Torah*]. You who want to be justified by the law [*Torah*] have cut yourselves off from Christ; you have fallen away from grace (Galatians 5:2-4).

Paul is trying with all of his considerable intellectual, rhetorical, and biblical abilities to turn the Galatians back to Christ. Because for Paul, theology matters. The teaching one receives is almost never neutral – it either leads one closer to Christ or further away from Christ. By insisting that the Galatian Christians be circumcised in order to come into line with the Jewish covenant, these teachers are marching these young Christians straight back into the condemnation of the law that Jesus had just saved them from!

DID THE EARLY CHURCH PRACTISE TITHING?

But let's follow the evidence one step further. Almost all of the earliest Christians were Jews. So even if the new Gentile Christians were not required to follow the law, were these Jewish Christians meant to give a 23.3 per cent tithe just as Jews did under the covenant made at Sinai?

The examples of Christians in action in the book of Acts seem to indicate that they actually gave quite a lot more than even a Jewish tithe! These first Christians don't seem very interested in percentages. It may surprise you to know that the word *tithe(s)* appears 28 times across the Old Testament, but it appears only a few times in the entire New Testament, usually referring to Jews still trying to observe the *Torah*. Tithing is never commanded for New Testament believers.[6]

These early believers took Jesus's radical teachings on stewardship seriously. It is interesting that the amount Christians should give is not addressed in any of the literature that survives from the first century and a half of Christianity. This suggests that whatever Christians were doing, there was no controversy about it. They were simply following the practice handed down from Jesus and the apostles. Nowhere do we see any Christian leader, from the apostles themselves to their successors, the bishops, teaching that Christians must continue to practise tithing in the same way as under the Old Covenant.

The first clear record we have of what the early church taught about Old Testament tithing comes from the second century. Irenaeus, the Bishop of Lyon (in what today is southern France), wrote down what seems to be the standard procedure of Christian churches in both the West and the East. Like the examples we see in Acts, Irenaeus believed Christians were called to be stewards, not to tithe. We might expect that the early church's view of stewardship was too impractical and would fade away after the first generation. Instead, we find succeeding generations of Christians with the same motivation and practice when it comes to their wealth and possessions. Instead of a moderated view of Christian giving, Irenaeus astonishes us by matter-of-factly explaining a radical understanding of stewardship (emphasis mine):

> Therefore the offering of the church, which the Lord directed to be offered in the whole world, is accounted a pure sacrifice with God, and is acceptable to him, not that he needs a sacrifice from us, but because he who offers is himself honoured in his offering if his gift be accepted. By his offering, both honour and affection are shown to the King. And our Lord taught us to offer this in all simplicity and innocence (Matthew 5:23, 24). Therefore, we must offer to God the first fruits of his creation, as Moses said. Offerings are no longer

> offered by bondsmen, but by free men . . . They [OT saints] offered their tithes; *but those who have received liberty set apart everything they have for the Lord's use,* cheerfully and freely giving them (2 Corinthians 9:7), not as small things in the hope of greater, but like that poor widow, who put her whole livelihood into the treasury of God (Luke 21:4).[7]

Irenaeus acknowledges the requirement to tithe under the Old Covenant, but he also asserts that the New Covenant community is under no such obligation. Instead, love carries no limit – Christians will share everything they have with those in need. Whether or not there were Christians who carried on the old practice of tithing, Irenaeus says Christians were operating under a new concept of stewardship and living under a new regime of generosity. As we shall see in the next chapter, Christ calls us to put everything we have at God's disposal.

Tithing was part of God's covenant with Israel on Mount Sinai. But nobody was able to keep that covenant. That is why the Messiah had to save his people and open the way of salvation for the rest of the nations as well. The Old Testament points us to the Messiah, and the New Testament introduces us to the Lord Jesus, who calls us to a new and radical life. Jesus himself is the one who introduces us to the concept of stewardship – which may amount to much more than 10 per cent!

Living as if we are under the Old Covenant erodes the church's understanding and proclamation of the gospel.

Subsequent generations of Christians up to our own day have forgotten what the apostles taught us about the Old Testament. In spite of Paul's teaching in his letter to the Galatian Christians who were struggling with this very issue, eager Christian teachers keep trying today to impose requirements from the Old Covenant on people and churches who are instead under the New Covenant. Living as if we are under the Old Covenant erodes the church's understanding and proclamation of the gospel. As we will see in the next chapter, when we realize that everything we have is a gift from God, we will not need a law to tell us to give. Indeed, people will know we are true disciples of Christ by how we freely surrender these resources to be used for God's purposes.

BIBLE STUDY THREE

IS TITHING FOR CHRISTIANS?

After Gentiles began coming to faith in Christ, the early church faced a burning issue: Are Christians Jews? Are they under the covenant God made with Israel at Mount Sinai? This controversy threatened to destroy the new church. Some Jewish Christians forced new Gentile converts to be circumcised and keep the Old Testament commandments. Paul and his missionary companions taught that God was creating a new way to be reconciled through Christ rather than through the law. If you want to read how Christian leaders in Jerusalem came together to resolve this dispute, read Acts 15.

For this study, we will focus on the theology motivating the decision of the early Christian leaders, explained in Paul's letter to the church in Galatia. In this passage, "law" refers to the *Torah* or the covenant that God made with Israel at Mount Sinai, recorded in the first five books of the Bible.

Galatians 3:5-14

5 Well then, does God supply you with the Spirit and work miracles
among you by your doing the works of the law, or by your believing
what you heard?

6 Just as Abraham 'believed God, and it was reckoned to him as
righteousness', 7 so, you see, those who believe are the descendants of
Abraham. 8 And the scripture, foreseeing that God would justify the
Gentiles by faith, declared the gospel beforehand to Abraham, saying,
'All the Gentiles shall be blessed in you.' 9 For this reason, those who
believe are blessed with Abraham who believed.

10 For all who rely on the works of the law are under a curse; for it is
written, 'Cursed is everyone who does not observe and obey all the
things written in the book of the law.' 11 Now it is evident that no one is

justified before God by the law; for 'The one who is righteous will live
by faith.'[12] But the law does not rest on faith; on the contrary, 'Whoever
does the works of the law will live by them.'[13] Christ redeemed us from
the curse of the law by becoming a curse for us – for it is written,
'Cursed is everyone who hangs on a tree' – [14] in order that in Christ
Jesus the blessing of Abraham might come to the Gentiles, so that we
might receive the promise of the Spirit through faith.

Questions to Discuss

1. Some Jewish Christians argued that, in order to be truly saved, Gentile believers needed to become Jewish by being circumcised and following the law. Why was this wrong, according to Paul?
2. According to verses 10-14, what is the problem for everyone who tries to have a right relationship with God by keeping the law God gave to Israel? How did Jesus solve this problem?
3. How can both Jews and Gentiles be restored to fellowship with God?
4. Since tithing was part of the Old Covenant and its commandments, what does this passage have to say to Christians about tithing?
5. Can you think of a time you or your church have tried to give to God or obey the law to earn his favour? How does this new insight affect your attitude?
6. Sing or pray together, praising God for how Jesus has redeemed us from the curse of the law!

CHAPTER FOUR

SELL ALL YOU HAVE AND GIVE TO THE POOR

Have you ever noticed how often Jesus talked about money? Of his 39 parables, 11 are about financial priorities and stewardship. Jesus talked more about money than he did about heaven and hell combined.

ALMSGIVING IN THE FIRST CENTURY

Jesus was a first-century Jew, so his teachings came in a context that is unfamiliar to many of us. Let's take a few minutes to better understand Jesus in his own setting. All good first-century Jews were expected to give to people in need. The Jewish Scriptures urge both leaders and people to "remember the poor". God promised to bless them if they were generous instead of stingy by giving or lending to the poor (Deuteronomy 15:7-8, 10-11). They were to give because giving is an aspect of who God is. He is a God who executes justice for the orphan and the widow and provides for the resident alien (Deuteronomy 10:18).

They were to give because giving is an aspect of who God is.

Giving to the poor or "almsgiving" is so closely tied to right relationships that in the Talmud and in the later rabbinic literature they are referred to simply as *zedakah* – righteousness (via Arabic, *zedekah* metamorphosed into the Swahili word *sadaka* – offering).[8] Perhaps surprisingly to our ears, the rabbis understood charity not so much as a kindness to the poor person but as something to which they were *entitled,* and the giver was thus *obligated* to give. As one rabbi wrote, "The poor man does more for the householder (in accepting alms) than the householder does for the poor man (by giving him the charity)", because he is giving the householder the opportunity to do something good.[9]

The idea was that everyone's things belong to God and that poverty and riches come from God. The rabbis further state in *Avot* (3:8): "Give unto him of what is his, seeing that you and what you have are his." In other words, when one gives to the poor, one is giving not what belongs to oneself but what belongs to the Lord, and thus to the poor. God blesses those who have so that they, in turn, can be God's blessing to those who have not.

JESUS'S MANIFESTO ON MONEY

There are many similarities between what Jesus teaches in the Gospels and what one finds in the Torah and in later rabbinic teaching about almsgiving and stewardship. In Jesus's manifesto for discipleship, the so-called Sermon on the Mount, in Matthew 5–7, he explains God's intentions underlying the Jewish law. But Jesus explains that these ancient Jewish emphases require a heart transformation. Stewardship in Jesus's hands becomes a lens through which one's heart comes into focus. Stewardship becomes the way we fulfil the greatest commandments, how we love God with all our heart, how we love our neighbour as ourselves.

This passage gives today's Christians guidance about how to apply these Old Covenant concerns to our New Covenant lives. When it comes to giving to the poor, Jesus says "*when* you give alms." He *assumes that his followers will be giving*. His concern, instead, is that giving should be done not with an eye to impress the wider society but done secretly. People who give to win others' praise have been rewarded already, but God will reward any giving done in secret (Matthew 6:1-4).

Almost every African culture has fundraising events that provide the wealthy with a stage for flaunting both their wealth and their giving. In Kenya, *harambees* began as a cultural practice to help local communities pool together to build a school or meet a local need. Many churches now use *harambees* to raise the large sums of money that are needed for purchasing land, building structures, or other large projects. Invitations are sent to wealthy individuals and politicians. In meetings after the worship service, individuals come to the front, where their donations are announced to everyone.

Jesus rather bluntly questions such self-serving displays. He directs his followers to address need in ways that do not draw attention to themselves.[10] In most cultures, money and the way it is used is the main way to exercise power. For Jesus, money is not to be an instrument of power, but of compassion. Therefore, money and possessions are not to be accumulated for the sake of having more and more, or as a demonstration to everyone else of how successful or blessed a person is. Instead, if I have an abundance of wealth and a lot of stuff, God has given those resources to me for a reason. My treasure is to be used not for myself or for advancing personal agendas, but for the common good. Next, Jesus makes the uncomfortable observation that the way one uses money and "stores up treasure" is a straightforward revelation of the orientation of one's heart, "For where your treasure is, there your heart will be also . . . No one can serve two masters; for a slave will either hate the one and love the other, or be devoted to one and despise the other. You cannot serve God and wealth" (Matthew 6:21, 24 NRSV-A).

Jesus is warning us that greed is dangerous. This reminds me of Crabtree Falls, a beautiful series of waterfalls in the United States where people hike and picnic. Signs are posted everywhere warning people not to venture into the water. But some people believe they are strong enough to avoid any danger. What could go wrong by wading in a bit? But when they get into the stream, they find a faster current and more slippery rocks than they anticipated. At least 30 people have died in the last four decades, swept over the edge of the waterfall.

Jesus's words about greed and riches are like the signs warning hikers that what seems beautiful is actually deadly. Yet we often ignore the warnings, thinking they don't apply to us. "I want to make money," we think, "as long as I do it honestly and attend church, it can't hurt." But Jesus is serious when he says we can't serve two masters. Do we trust him to know the danger?

THE RICH YOUNG RULER

One of the most disturbing incidents in the Gospels is Jesus's conversation with a wealthy young man who wanted to know what he needed to do to gain eternal life (or "be saved"). The man said he had kept all of the commandments, so Jesus told him: "There is still one thing lacking. Sell all that you own and distribute the money to the poor, and you will have treasure in heaven; then come, follow me" (Luke 18:22).

"Surely Jesus cannot be serious," we clamour. The disciples too were astonished at how this conversation turned out. They watched the rich man walk sadly away, thinking that following Jesus cost too much. Perhaps the disciples thought to themselves: "The guy has lots of money.

He would have made an excellent member of the team. He could have bankrolled your biggest projects, Jesus!"

Jesus did not help matters with his next statement: "Indeed, it is easier for a camel to go through the eye of a needle than for someone who is rich to enter the kingdom of God" (Luke 18:25). Not only did this clash with his followers' understanding of salvation, it demonstrated rather nicely that Jesus was much bigger than the box they were attempting to put him in. "Those who heard this said, 'Then who can be saved?' " (Luke 18:26).

Jesus reminded them just what an impossible reach salvation is: "He replied, 'What is impossible for mortals is possible for God' " (Luke 18:27). Salvation *is* hard; it is a narrow way, as opposed to the broad highway most would rather travel. It is hard precisely because it touches and intends to transform, all of our values, including the way we view and use our possessions. Repentance requires radical changes in every human heart, in putting off our old rebellion and putting on Christ and his priorities instead. It is impossible for any of us to do this on our own.

This radical surgery Jesus prescribed for this wealthy young man was shocking. It's similar to the radical surgery, chemotherapy, and radiation treatment inflicted on someone who has a life-threatening cancer. Jesus knew the young man was sick, and his illness was life-threatening. So Jesus said: "Sell what you have and give the money to the poor."

More than a few Christians believe the opposite is true. Ostentatious wealth and prosperity, they say, are a sign of God's blessing. Everyone should seek more and more wealth. Lack of such "blessing" means you are missing out on what God wants to do for you. These Christians are often quick to say that the rich man's wealth was not the problem.

Our desire to accumulate wealth becomes a life-threatening cancer that will destroy us if left to run its course.

Jesus, however, knows better. He seems to know precisely when our desire to accumulate wealth becomes a life-threatening cancer that will destroy us if left to run its course. Jesus's question to the wealthy young man was essentially: "Which is more important to you, keeping your wealth or following me?"

The young man was, like many of us, likely hoping for a third option – "Both!" But that was not offered. While the call to let go of our wealth may seem unnecessary to us, Jesus, who knows our hearts, knows the danger we are in. He knows that it's not just wealth and possessions that rust and corrode and get stolen; human hearts rust and corrode and get stolen. He knows our hearts become corrupt when wealth is accumulated and spent only on ourselves. Jesus knows that wealth tends to distract those who possess it from true life and meaning.

THE RICH YOUNG EGYPTIAN

This story from the Gospels reminds me of an Egyptian named Anthony, who was born in the mid-third century to wealthy land-owning Christian parents. When he was 20, both his parents died. As the only son, Anthony inherited the entire estate. Shortly afterwards, in church, Anthony heard about Jesus's conversation with the rich young man. Anthony felt he was the young man Jesus was addressing. He promptly arranged for his young sister to be cared for by a group of Christian women, and then he sold his estate and gave the proceeds to help the needy and the poor.

At this point, Anthony heard Christ's call to follow him into the desert to pray. While there had been other Christian men who had fled to the desert to pursue a life of solitude, poverty, and prayer, Anthony's example spurred a movement of both men and women to take seriously Jesus's claims of discipleship in the face of the growing worldliness of the church.[11]

We know this movement today as monasticism, and God has used multitudes of these faithful men and women to preserve the church in times of peril and great darkness, as well as advancing the gospel across cultural and racial barriers. The impact of this young Egyptian's obedience is still being felt today, 1,700 years later.

CHANGED HEARTS

The parable of the sheep and the goats in Matthew 25 is one of the few times Jesus addresses the final judgement that every person must face. During that final judgement, Jesus doesn't ask about miracles performed or religious services attended. He doesn't even ask about how many people we evangelized! The Judge's concern, rather, is whether people fed the hungry, clothed the poor, and cared for the sick and imprisoned. In fact, the Judge takes it so personally that it is as if they failed to care for him: "Truly I tell you, just as you did not do it to the least of these, you did not do it to me" (Matthew 25:45).

Jesus, the One before whom you and I must give an account, is not concerned about the things that vex most Christians and churches. Instead, he will be asking: "What have you done with the time, talents, and resources that I entrusted to you?" Specifically, this passage teaches us that our salvation will be demonstrated by how we served the poor and needy.

I sometimes wonder if the fear of using good works to earn our salvation has destroyed any motive for us Christians to work any good at all with our resources. Good works save no one. But one who has been reconciled to God through faith and repentance *will,* by the power of the Holy Spirit, become a fountain of good works – of love, of mercy, of generosity. In other words, our salvation transforms us into the good stewards Jesus calls us to be.

Instead, Zacchaeus changed his life because he had met Jesus.

When Jesus said to Zacchaeus: "Today salvation has come to your house," it was because Zacchaeus had repented. He had changed his priorities, his agenda, his behaviour, and his life. He gave half of what he had to the poor, and to those whom he had defrauded, he restored fourfold what he had taken (Luke 19:1-10). Did Zacchaeus *have* to do these things in order to be saved? There is nothing in this story to indicate that earning salvation was the issue. Instead, Zacchaeus changed his life because he had met Jesus.

If we are genuinely born again, then we will bear a family likeness with our Older Brother and our Heavenly Father. As the apostle John put it: "Beloved, we are God's children now; what we will be has not yet been revealed. What we do know is this: when he is revealed, we will be like him, for we will see him as he is. And all who have this hope in him purify themselves, just as he is pure" (1 John 3:2-3).

We demonstrate the reality of our faith, of our relationship with Christ, not with our religious words but by the way we love God and love our neighbours. If we are saved and are following Jesus as his disciples, it will be obvious from our joyful stewardship.

BIBLE STUDY FOUR

SELL ALL YOU HAVE AND GIVE TO THE POOR

Jesus's teaching about money and possessions shocked the people who listened to him in the first century, just as his words continue to shock people today who take the time to hear what he is saying. He has more to say about money than about anything else, and he is not interested in giving comfort to those who are content with the status quo. Rather, Jesus knows that what we do with our possessions clearly indicates what is happening in our hearts. And the spiritual health of our hearts is a matter of eternal life and death. If Jesus sounds dramatic when he talks about stewardship, it is because he's trying to wake us up.

Let's look more closely at one of Jesus's strong statements of the importance of stewardship in eternal perspective. He is telling this story as a parable about the final judgement at the end of the age.

Matthew 25:31-46

31 'When the Son of Man comes in his glory, and all the angels with
him, then he will sit on the throne of his glory. 32 All the nations will be
gathered before him, and he will separate people one from another as
a shepherd separates the sheep from the goats, 33 and he will put the
sheep at his right hand and the goats at the left. 34 Then the king will
say to those at his right hand, "Come, you that are blessed by my
Father, inherit the kingdom prepared for you from the foundation of
the world; 35 for I was hungry and you gave me food, I was thirsty and
you gave me something to drink, I was a stranger and you welcomed
me, 36 I was naked and you gave me clothing, I was sick and you took
care of me, I was in prison and you visited me." 37 Then the righteous
will answer him, "Lord, when was it that we saw you hungry and gave
you food, or thirsty and gave you something to drink? 38 And when
was it that we saw you a stranger and welcomed you, or naked and
gave you clothing? 39 And when was it that we saw you sick or in prison

and visited you?" 40 And the king will answer them, "Truly I tell you, just as you did it to one of the least of these who are members of my family, you did it to me." 41 Then he will say to those at his left hand, "You that are accursed, depart from me into the eternal fire prepared for the devil and his angels; 42 for I was hungry and you gave me no food, I was thirsty and you gave me nothing to drink, 43 I was a stranger and you did not welcome me, naked and you did not give me clothing, sick and in prison and you did not visit me." 44 Then they also will answer, "Lord, when was it that we saw you hungry or thirsty or a stranger or naked or sick or in prison, and did not take care of you?"
45 Then he will answer them, "Truly I tell you, just as you did not do it to one of the least of these, you did not do it to me." 46 And these will go away into eternal punishment, but the righteous into eternal life.'

Questions to Discuss

1. In the parable, who must stand before Jesus?
2. What are the criteria which Jesus will use to judge? What will be the difference between the people on his right and on his left?
3. Jesus will call all the people on his right "blessed". Based on the passage, what does this blessing involve?
4. Jesus will criticize the people on his left for what they have not done. They will seem surprised and shocked. Why?
5. The words *salvation* and *stewardship* are not mentioned in this parable, but they are the unspoken themes of the entire drama. What do we learn about salvation from this parable? What do we learn about stewardship from this parable?
6. As a group, pray and ask the Holy Spirit: who in our community needs food, water, a warm welcome, clothes, or a visit?

CHAPTER FIVE

TRUST GOD WITH YOUR FINANCIAL FUTURE

In the Sermon on the Mount, Jesus addresses one of our primary concerns, which is, "If I really trust God with everything I have, how do I know I won't run out of everything I need and just die?" Jesus responds to our deep-seated fear by talking about how we can live worry-free, like the birds in the sky and the flowers in the field (Matthew 6:25-33). Jesus's followers can be generous with what we have because we know that God – "your Father", as Jesus says – will take care of us just as he takes care of creation.

In Luke's version of the Sermon on the Mount, Jesus ends with these words: "Do not be afraid, little flock, for it is your Father's good pleasure to give you the kingdom. Sell your possessions and give alms" (Luke 12:32-33 NRSV-A). Being generous with our possessions is simply a matter of expressing our faith that God will take care of us, whereas worry and anxiety about possessions reveal a profound lack of trust in the God who made us and loves us.

BAPTIZED WITH HIS WALLET

As a young man, David Kasali was very worried about having adequate possessions. His father was a poor pastor in the Democratic Republic of Congo who had struggled to provide school fees and shoes for nine children on a ministry salary.[12] David resolved to work and study hard so he wouldn't be like his father. He got a good paying job and was entrusted with the company's funds.

At the bank where David deposited the company's funds, the bank manager befriended him. He invited him to prayer meetings, and David realized that Christianity was a love relationship with God. At one prayer meeting, a woman told David the Lord was calling him into full-time ministry, but he had been running away. David pulled out his wallet and said:

> This is why I have been running away. I wanted to work for my own life, to earn my own money. I wanted to be able to send my children to school. It is as though, when I was baptized, I pulled my wallet out of my pocket and said, 'Don't baptize my wallet.' Today, I want my wallet to be baptized with me. I surrender it.

"Today, I want my wallet to be baptized with me."

From that point, David's life completely changed. Now, he wanted to be like his father, totally surrendered to God in trusting dependence. David left his job and moved his family to a remote village to teach high school students and disciple them. While there, he received a scholarship to study at the Nairobi Evangelical Graduate School of Theology (NEGST, today part of Africa International University). After that, he got the opportunity to work and travel throughout Africa with the Association of Evangelicals in Africa, which left him with many questions about Christianity in Africa. He pursued these questions in his doctoral studies in the US, then returned to teach at NEGST, where soon afterwards he became the Vice Chancellor.

But yet again, David didn't pursue his own ambition. Troubled by the violence affecting his people in the Democratic Republic of the Congo, he prayerfully quit that post. He moved back to the conflict zone to be with his people and discern what the church could do. Out of those conversations, he founded a bilingual Christian university that has been a beacon of hope for the community, *l'Université Chrétienne Bilingue du Congo*. Reflecting on his life, David says:

> My life – the way I wanted it – was to be for the first few years in the university and in the business world. But from then on, my life was as the Lord wanted it, everything I was and everything that came to me was not me fighting for it, it was just God . . . My life was surrendered to God, and then he gave me back what I was passionate about . . . if I belonged to myself, I would still be struggling and sitting somewhere doing what, I do not know.

David trusted God to provide for himself and his family. He surrendered and lived a life devoted to God and others. As a result, God has been able to use him in amazing ways.

MORE BARNS, BIGGER AND BETTER!

Like any good teacher, Jesus makes his point in a variety of ways. And in doing so, he leaves no doubt as to what he is trying to say. The question is, are we willing to listen?

When someone asked Jesus to help him get his share of the inheritance from his brother, Jesus told another story. He described a man so rich that he built extra barns to store his harvest, expecting to relax and enjoy his wealth for years to come. But that very night, he died. He invested everything in this life instead of investing in God's priorities. In the perspective of eternity, his stockpile of possessions was useless, and he was a fool (Luke 12:13-21).

Now, the problem with the rich man and his productive farms was not that his fields were productive or that he was making money. Rather, the rich man was greedy. He considered his earnings to be *his* to use for his own pleasure. Jesus said: "Take care! Be on your guard against all kinds of greed; for one's life does not consist in the abundance of possessions" (Luke 12:15). Often, the rich are actually impoverished when it comes to the things of God. Any of the possessions treasured by people in this life can be evidence of resources and opportunities misused.

Instead of being God's slaves who manage all the things he has given us for his glory and the love of our neighbour, we can become slaves of our money and possessions. We can become bound to our culture's expectations of how successful people should live. So, we get our degrees, climb the job ladder, earn that salary, get that car, buy that house, and take that holiday to be seen by those people. But there is always more to acquire – a better job, salary, car, house, or holiday. There is always another barn to build, until we discover that we have wasted our lives focusing on ourselves, accumulating treasure we cannot take with us when our time is up.

Jesus's story teaches that all riches are God's, and they are given by him to be used for those things he considers important. Our wealth, opportunities, education, and skills are not ours, but have been given to us by God. So, the real question is not, "How much am I giving?" but "How well am I managing the resources entrusted to me by God?"

Take a moment and reflect. Are you spending what God has given you on yourself, your pleasures, and your agenda? Or are you focused on God's priorities and God's agendas? When opportunities come your way, do you use them for your advantage, or do you consider how you could use them for God?

FEEDING THE HUNGRY AND VISITING THE SICK

Sarah was an Ethiopian Christian whose husband got sick and died. At his funeral he was hailed as a good, honourable Christian man. Not long after his death however, Sarah got sick. A blood test showed that she was HIV-positive. Both her family and her husband's blamed her for her husband's death, but in fact, the husband had contracted HIV from visiting prostitutes, thereby infecting her and their unborn child. Because of the shame and stigma, he had never gotten tested; he didn't want to know. The relatives drove Sarah and her three children, including her HIV-positive newborn daughter, out of the house and onto the streets.

Having lost everything, she begged for food to feed her children. Members of the church where I served as senior pastor found them and gave them medical care from a team of visiting doctors. Our outreach ministry provided food and school fees for the older children. And they built a small but adequate house so Sarah and her family could have a roof over their heads.

Not long after this, the director and I went to visit Sarah and found her weak and unable to move in her bed. We thought she might be dying of AIDS. We laid our hands on her and I began praying: "In the name of Jesus . . ." She suddenly shrieked and snarled and violently thrashed about her bed. We held her down so she wouldn't hurt herself or us, and we prayed that God would deliver Sarah from what seemed to be a demonic attack. Sarah suddenly collapsed and lay still. We stayed for some time, and then left her in the care of her neighbours.

A few days later we were shocked to see Sarah walking into the director's office. She was praising God for delivering her from the demons and had come to thank us for praying for her.

Our church's practical ministry to someone who others ignored is an example of the kind of Christianity that distinguishes the sheep from the goats, and it is something any of us can do right where we are.

THE SUPREME EXAMPLE

No matter how much or how little we have, we can be stewards of what God has given us. God is not impressed with amounts given in his name, because a rich person can give a vast amount to be seen by others as generous, and yet he has not come close to giving sacrificially.

While teaching near the place in the Temple complex where offerings were brought, Jesus directed his disciples to watch carefully. Wealthy people put in large sums, but a poor widow put in only two coins. Jesus said: "Truly I tell you, this poor widow has put in more than all of them; for all of them have contributed out of their abundance, but she out of her poverty has put in all she had to live on" (Luke 21:3-4).

She gave what she had, not so that anyone would see her, but just to express to the Lord that she was his and trusting him to provide what she needed. Two copper coins made no significant increase whatsoever in the Temple's budget. But heaven had not seen a gift so substantial in a very long time.

THE ETHIOPIAN WIDOW'S GIFT

The story of the widow's gift at the Temple reminds me of what happened next with Sarah, the HIV-positive widow mentioned in the story above. About a month after Sarah was delivered from the demonic attack, a newborn baby was left at the church's gate. The infant was probably HIV-positive, which meant that nobody would want her. In those days, an HIV-positive child might live five or six years, but would grow sick and weak and inevitably die. Our ministry director circulated the need for someone who could care for this baby while we searched for a long-term solution.

The next day, Sarah came by the director's office again. "I want to take care of that little girl," she said.

"Why?" the director asked. "You already have three children to take care of."

"Yes," said Sarah, "but I know how to take care of children, even sick children. And besides, after all God has done for me, how can I not give what I have to take care of this little girl who desperately needs someone to love her and be a family for her?"

Sarah took the infant home. I have since moved from Ethiopia and have lost track of Sarah and her family. But she brings to life for me just what a poor widow's two mites can do. The poor woman who had nothing in the world's eyes is now showing people what love is, what gratitude does, and what it means to be a good steward.

IT ALL BELONGS TO GOD

What we see again and again in the Gospels is that Jesus wants to rescue us from the ways of this world and reclaim us for his kingdom. He knows if we persist in our love of money, we will destroy ourselves. Jesus's hard words about stewardship offer us the way of life on the narrow road to salvation. If our lives and churches are impoverished in the things of God, it is because, ironically, too many of us feel we have too much to lose if we take stewardship seriously.

Jesus lays claim to all of our lives and confronts us with the call to follow him.

Whether we call it the "lordship of Christ" or "stewardship", the biblical concept is precisely the same. Everything we have and everything we are belongs to Christ. Not just a few coins, not just 10 per cent, but *everything*. So, we need to use everything he places in our hands, every talent and ability, for the sake of his agenda and glory.

Jesus lays claim to all of our lives and confronts us with the call to follow him. The primary means by which we love both God and our neighbour is not with our words, but with what we have been given by God – our time and our talents and our treasure. This is why our relationship with our material possessions shows more clearly than any other indicator the true direction of our lives.

BIBLE STUDY FIVE

TRUST GOD WITH YOUR FINANCIAL FUTURE

Jesus tells parables, one of his most effective ways of driving home a point. These were not merely entertaining stories. He started with a story or a description of something everybody already knew, but he ended it in a way nobody expected. If the story was the bait, the ending was the hook that caught and drew one into the new reality that Jesus was describing. Jesus's parables still have the same effect today. When we listen closely, we are jolted into an awareness of something much bigger and better than our sin-constrained minds have allowed. The parable we will read now is a good example of Jesus at work, using a story to get our attention and then using his conclusion to turn our world upside down.

In the parable we are about to read together, Jesus tells about a man who has been fabulously successful.

Luke 12:13-24

> 13 Someone in the crowd said to [Jesus], 'Teacher, tell my brother to
> divide the family inheritance with me.' 14 But he said to him, 'Friend,
> who set me to be a judge or arbitrator over you?' 15 And he said to
> them, 'Take care! Be on your guard against all kinds of greed; for one's
> life does not consist in the abundance of possessions.' 16 Then he told
> them a parable: 'The land of a rich man produced abundantly. 17 And
> he thought to himself, "What should I do, for I have no place to store
> my crops?" 18 Then he said, "I will do this: I will pull down my barns and
> build larger ones, and there I will store all my grain and my goods.
> 19 And I will say to my soul, Soul, you have ample goods laid up for
> many years; relax, eat, drink, be merry." 20 But God said to him, "You
> fool! This very night your life is being demanded of you. And the
> things you have prepared, whose will they be?" 21 So it is with those
> who store up treasures for themselves but are not rich towards God.'

[22] He said to his disciples, 'Therefore I tell you, do not worry about your life, what you will eat, or about your body, what you will wear. [23] For life is more than food, and the body more than clothing. [24] Consider the ravens: they neither sow nor reap, they have neither storehouse nor barn, and yet God feeds them. Of how much more value are you than the birds!

Questions to Discuss

1. Why would many people in our communities and churches consider the rich man in Jesus's story blessed?
2. How does this parable's shocking ending challenge our idea of blessing?
3. How does Jesus's warning about saving up treasure for yourself compare to the financial advice in your culture?
4. According to this passage, how does a relationship with God enable us to have a different attitude about our finances and the future?
5. What examples does Jesus give in verses 31-34 of ways one can be rich towards God?
6. Spend some time confessing your attitude about finances to God. Ask the Holy Spirit to show you one way to invest more treasure in heaven this week.

CHAPTER SIX

SHARING ALL THINGS IN COMMON

When we say Jesus is our Lord, it means fully surrendering to Christ. The Christians in Acts recognized that their lives were no longer their own – everything they were and had was a gift from God.

Jesus's teaching about stewardship was not an idealized version that the first Christians quickly dismissed. The early Christians did not feel at liberty to ignore the aspects of Jesus's teaching they didn't like. Instead, in their lives and communities they earnestly attempted to reproduce Jesus's teachings about money and stewardship, passed on to them by the apostles.

Luke's summary statements in the early chapters of Acts are striking:

> They devoted themselves to the apostles' teaching and fellowship, to the breaking of bread and the prayers.
>
> Awe came upon everyone, because many wonders and signs were being done by the apostles. All who believed were together and had all things in common; they would sell their possessions and goods and distribute the proceeds to all, as any had need. Day by day, as they spent much time together in the temple, they broke bread at home and ate their food with glad and generous hearts, praising God and having the goodwill of all the people. And day by day the Lord added to their number those who were being saved (Acts 2:42-47 NRSV-A).

And again, after some time had passed:

> Now the whole group of those who believed were of one heart and soul, and no one claimed private ownership of any possessions, but everything they owned was held in common. With great power the apostles gave their testimony to the resurrection of the Lord Jesus, and great grace was upon them all. There was not a needy person

among them, for as many as owned lands or houses sold them and brought the proceeds of what was sold. They laid it at the apostles' feet and it was distributed to each as any had need (Acts 4:32-35).

It is easy for us to pick our way carefully through these passages to avoid their impact. For example, F. Scott Spencer writes, "Of course, however much we might admire the radical communitarian practice of the early Jerusalem church, we may also pity, even decry, their shortsighted, impractical economic vision. Quite possibly, it contributed to hard times down the line, requiring assistance (bailout) from the more prosperous congregation in Antioch (11:27-30)." Yet Spencer still ends by warning that dismissing the early church's practice risks "dismissing their vibrant resurrection faith that ignited their extraordinary common-fellowship *(koinonia)* in the first place. And resurrection faith that does not profoundly shape communal practice lacks depth of meaning and breadth of appeal."[13]

Depending on our political leanings, we might also disparage the practices of the early Jerusalem church by associating them with communism.[14] For instance, Jason Jackson is quick to clarify that unlike a Marxist-forced redistribution of wealth, the members of the church still owned pieces of land or homes and sold property voluntarily. The property was distributed to the needy – not everyone, and not people who refused to work.[15] But Jackson's concerns are based on comparing these practices with a secular economic theory that didn't emerge for another 1,800 years.

If we dismiss the community life of a first-century church because we think it's too similar to economic and political ideologies from the 19th and 20th centuries, we are ignorant at best. At worst, we are trying to justify not taking seriously the example of the first Christians.[16]

Of the many things that could be said about these passages, one thing stands out: What these first Christians were doing was completely consistent with what Jesus had been teaching just a few months before. In other words, the Jerusalem church was not suddenly devising a new economic policy. Rather, the community was motivated by one driving concern – to give help to the needy among them.[17] And a straight line can be drawn from their concern for the poor back to Jesus himself. They took seriously what Jesus had said the night he was betrayed: "I give you a new commandment, that you love one another. Just as I have loved you, you also should love one another. By this everyone will know that you are my disciples, if you have love for one another" (John 13:34-35).

What these first Christians were doing was completely consistent with what Jesus had been teaching just a few months before.

And so, when they came across instances of need within the community, they took steps to help. As a result, "There was not a needy person among them" (Acts 4:34a). Given the size of the early Christian movement, this is quite a remarkable thing for Luke to say.

Luke gives a specific example of this radical giving: "There was a Levite, a native of Cyprus, Joseph, to whom the apostles gave the name Barnabas (which means 'son of encouragement'). He sold a field that belonged to him, then brought the money and laid it at the apostles' feet" (Acts 4:36-37). We don't know how many in the Jerusalem church were choosing to give in this way. We also don't know the extent of the need in the Jerusalem church, nor do we know if the help they received went beyond food and rent to help people also find work and affordable housing. What we do know is that the help given by the Jerusalem Christians was substantial and that it met the needs of the community, though at considerable cost.

Relatively early on, the church created a methodology to ensure that none of the truly needy in the church were overlooked. But the day came when, despite their best efforts, some among them were overlooked; widows amongst the Hellenist Christians "were being neglected in the daily distribution" (Acts 6:1). First of all it's worth noticing that there *was* a daily distribution for the needy in the community. Anyone who has worked in a soup kitchen or a food pantry for the poor knows the level of organization and effort required to be effective.

Second, it took so much effort that the apostles came to admit that they could not continue to run the ministry themselves. Grumblings that Greek-speaking widows were being overlooked in the distribution of food were taken seriously. The apostles were evidently stretched thin and overwhelmed. Moreover, the burden of administering charity was so significant that the apostles felt they were being increasingly kept from their mission of evangelism and teaching.

Hence a new level of community leadership was created to take responsibility for the programmes that would implement Jesus's teaching about love, giving, and the poor. The selection of deacons in Acts 6 indicates the extent of the charity being practised by the Jerusalem community.[18] Considering that seven men were selected to administer this ministry, we can see just how substantial the church's effort was to take care of the needy in Jerusalem.

This was not a momentary emphasis of the first Christians. The apostles were focused and serious about facilitating the care of the marginalized among them throughout their lives. And it required more than just individual charity; the entire community was mobilized to see this as a crucial aspect of their discipleship and their mission as a church.

CALLED TO LOVE

The church in Acts demonstrates that as we become more like Jesus, we begin to see the world around us through Jesus's eyes. Our hearts begin to fill up with the love he has for the poor and the lost.

Jesus calls his followers to love each other in the same way that he loves them. Love is the engine that drives stewardship. Self-giving love stops and helps, even if it is inconvenient. Love gives quietly, without attracting attention to itself, to help someone needy. Love takes time with the widows and orphans, feeds the hungry, visits the forgotten in prison, and cares for the sick and dying. Love intentionally mobilizes what we have and who we are for the sake of another.

One of the most influential prayers a person can pray is to ask, "Lord, open my eyes. Help me to see the people around me as you see them. Help me to love the people around me as you love them." This is a prayer that God loves to answer. This is a prayer that we stewards pray as we are seeking the Lord's will about what to do with our time, with our things, and with our money.

"Lord, open my eyes. Help me to see the people around me as you see them. Help me to love the people around me as you love them."

God will answer prayers like this, coming from the hearts of men and women who love God and want to love their neighbour. When he does, our churches will change. They will exist no longer just for our benefit, our entertainment, or our comfort. Instead we will see that our reason for existence is to become the love of Jesus where we are.

As Acts reminds us, we can only love in community. So it is of vital importance that we are in a church community of like-minded disciples. Just as a seed needs the right conditions to grow, it helps for us to find a community where we can grow spiritually and become more and more like Christ. Perhaps you need to join a church where people are excited about following Jesus wholeheartedly. Within the body of Christ, we grow in our commitment to stewardship, to following Jesus in every aspect of our lives. We then become the churches where the Kingdom of God is breaking into our world.

FEEDING THE HUNGRY

When we pray to see people as God sees them and get our community involved, we can witness radical transformation like that recorded in the early church. I knew of a church where a woman happened to be studying the Book of Acts during her personal Bible study and prayer time. When she read in chapter 6 about how the apostles dealt with the need to better administer the Jerusalem church's charitable ministries to the poor in their midst, she realized their church could be spending its resources more faithfully in this regard. She soon came up with a plan.

First, she got the church board's permission to use the church's kitchen facilities and one of its Sunday school classrooms to start a healthy meal centre that would provide a hot, nutritious lunch every Wednesday. She recruited several other church ladies to volunteer their time and prepare the meals. She and another friend put up the money for the first month. They advertised by word of mouth, asking church members to invite the elderly, the infirm, and any poor people they knew, from within the church or outside it, to come and share a free meal on Wednesday at noon.

On the first Wednesday, to everyone's surprise, 20 people came. The next week the number doubled, and the kitchen staff struggled to have enough for everyone. The third week, nearly 80 came. They had to open two more classrooms to make room for everybody. By this time, church members were responding with offerings; others contributed plates and utensils and cups. More people volunteered to help the mamas in the kitchen. By the end of the first month, not only were more than 100 of the city's disadvantaged people coming to the church on Wednesday for lunch, but nearly 20 church members were mobilized to plan, shop, prepare, serve, and clean up.

When the woman who had started all this looked over the crowd of people sitting in classrooms and outside on the ground eating their lunch and others in line patiently waiting to be served, she suddenly realized what she was looking at. No longer was she seeing poor people, instead she saw men who were unemployed needing a hand to get through this hard time. She saw young mothers with infants in their arms and small children in tow, grateful for a warm, filling meal. She saw street boys who, at least for an hour, had something positive to focus on. She saw elderly women who came at the insistence of their neighbours, both to get out of the house and also get something healthy to eat. She saw other men who were notorious town drunks, but who in this hour at least put off their addiction and had positive contact with other people. All of them were fellow human beings – and by helping them, the church was fulfilling its calling.

The elders were astonished at the impact of a simple meal on both the lives of a growing circle of people and on the church. Several of them volunteered their time and money. The wife of an elder volunteered her time as a counsellor and began to meet with whoever wanted to talk. She was soon so overwhelmed by the sheer numbers of people wanting help with their challenges that she talked several of her colleagues into volunteering some hours every week to come and help.

By the end of the year, the board of elders had constructed a new kitchen big enough to handle the number of meals being prepared. They also built a large hall that could accommodate the large number of people who showed up. They brought on a director to better organize the process and provided offices for five or six counsellors to use. And they began serving lunch on Fridays as well. Church members and leaders were encouraged to simply come and get to know a new person every week. The poor or struggling in the community knew that on Wednesday and Friday they could get not only a hot meal, but they could come to a safe place where they were not judged but rather accepted as fellow human beings created in the image of God.

It is so easy for us to read what happened in the early church and to say, "That's impractical. God doesn't want our church doing that today."

But that was not how this woman reacted when she read Acts 6. She knew she was part of the same eternal church and served the same God. She trusted that he would equip her as she stepped out in radical faith. What would happen if we took the example of the early church seriously and decided to do something?

BIBLE STUDY SIX

SHARING ALL THINGS IN COMMON

We have seen that Jesus did not shy away from teaching about material possessions and stewardship. In the last study, we saw Jesus explain in detail what it means to be "rich towards God". Now let's look at how the early Christians put his teaching into practice.

Many of the first Christians in Jerusalem had likely heard Jesus teach and preach. His execution was a public event, thanks to Roman cruelty. Jesus had risen again from the dead and presented himself alive to many witnesses. The Kingdom of God had spectacularly broken into human history and they were now all part of that kingdom. The gospel resulted in a new way of living, a way marked by loving God and loving one's neighbour. How they treated one another and used their resources increasingly proclaimed that they were created in the image of God and saved by Jesus. The Holy Spirit was at work in their midst, touching every part of their lives and their priorities. In two passages from Acts, we see the effects on how they used their money, property, and resources.

Acts 2:40-47

> 40 And [Peter] testified with many other arguments and exhorted
> them, saying, 'Save yourselves from this corrupt generation.' 41 So
> those who welcomed his message were baptized, and that day about
> three thousand persons were added. 42 They devoted themselves to
> the apostles' teaching and fellowship, to the breaking of bread and
> the prayers.
>
> 43 Awe came upon everyone, because many wonders and signs were
> being done by the apostles. 44 All who believed were together and had
> all things in common; 45 they would sell their possessions and goods
> and distribute the proceeds to all, as any had need. 46 Day by day, as
> they spent much time together in the temple, they broke bread at

home and ate their food with glad and generous hearts, [47] praising God and having the goodwill of all the people. And day by day the Lord added to their number those who were being saved.

Acts 4:32-37

[32] Now the whole group of those who believed were of one heart and
soul, and no one claimed private ownership of any possessions, but
everything they owned was held in common. [33] With great power the
apostles gave their testimony to the resurrection of the Lord Jesus, and
great grace was upon them all. [34] There was not a needy person among
them, for as many as owned lands or houses sold them and brought the
proceeds of what was sold. [35] They laid it at the apostles' feet, and it was
distributed to each as any had need. [36] There was a Levite, a native of
Cyprus, Joseph, to whom the apostles gave the name Barnabas (which
means 'son of encouragement'). [37] He sold a field that belonged to him,
then brought the money, and laid it at the apostles' feet.

Questions to Discuss

1. What are the Christians in Acts 2 and 4 doing that indicate they were taking Jesus's teaching about stewardship seriously?
2. What were some of the consequences of how the Christians were using their material and monetary possessions?
3. Why were these Christians motivated to have "everything in common"? What was the purpose and goal of this sharing?
4. What makes us hesitate to live this way today? Do you think these concerns are valid reasons or excuses?
5. Imagine together what your church and community would look like if you had the attitude of these early Christians. Can you describe what that might look and feel like?

CHAPTER SEVEN

CARING FOR THE GLOBAL BODY

We have seen that in Jerusalem, the church prioritised creating an effective administrative system, but it was a challenge. Shortly after this, the book of Acts describes how persecution scattered the Jerusalem church, and the Christian movement spread. Former persecutor Saul converted, and the rest of Acts describes Saul, who took the name Paul, as he travelled as a missionary and established churches throughout the Gentile Roman world. Paul's letters to these churches show that funding was also an issue for their new and growing churches, just as it is for most churches today.

Funding was also an issue for their new and growing churches, just as it is for most churches today.

The transition from pagan assumptions and a Greek worldview was challenging for the new Gentile Christians across the Mediterranean. It included a necessary change in mindset towards money, generosity, and stewardship. Most of the apostolic input on giving and stewardship occurred when the community was gathered to hear the apostles teach, or to hear their letters read. These covered the entire range of Christian issues, from Jesus and the gospel, to worship and sacraments, and matters of appropriate conduct and living out one's faith.

We learn from Paul's letter to the Romans that the church in Jerusalem had been enduring a particularly difficult time. He informed the Roman Christians that, before he could visit them in Rome, he had to go to Jerusalem:

> I do hope to see you on my journey [when I go to Spain] and to be sent on by you, once I have enjoyed your company for a little while. At present, however, I am going to Jerusalem in a ministry to the saints; for

> Macedonia and Achaia have been pleased to share their resources with the poor among the saints at Jerusalem (Romans 15:24-26 NRSV-A).

We learn from Paul's correspondence with the church in Corinth that not a little persuasion was necessary to motivate them to participate. Near the end of his first letter he wrote:

> Now concerning the collection for the saints: you should follow the directions I gave to the churches of Galatia. On the first day of every week, each of you is to put aside and save whatever extra you earn, so that collections need not be taken when I come. And when I arrive, I will send any whom you approve with letters to take your gift to Jerusalem. If it seems advisable that I should go also, they will accompany me (1 Corinthians 16:1-4).

But as the time drew near to actually collect the money and deliver it to Jerusalem, Paul found he needed to nudge the Corinthians to follow through on what they evidently had agreed to do. Here is Paul's undergirding principle, presumably with all the Greek churches, on this issue of stewardship:

> The point is this: the one who sows sparingly will also reap sparingly, and the one who sows bountifully will also reap bountifully. Each of you must give as you have made up your mind, not reluctantly or under compulsion, for God loves a cheerful giver. And God is able to provide you with every blessing in abundance, so that by always having enough of everything, you may share abundantly in every good work. As it is written,
>
> "He scatters abroad, he gives to the poor,
> his righteousness endures forever" (2 Corinthians 9:6-9).

The principle of sowing and reaping has been misused among preachers and ministers nowadays to encourage congregants to give money to their ministries. They say that the more people give ("sow") the more they will get ("reap"). Congregants give large amounts of money, expecting multiples in financial returns, or a lucrative business deal, or success in all their endeavours as "interest" on their investment. But this takes New Testament teaching on money out of context and makes our stewardship into simply another way to get access to money. For Jesus and Paul, it's not about using God to get rich, it's about giving as a way to demonstrate love, and without any hope of any return other than gratitude. We cannot manipulate God into making us wealthy. What Paul is trying to say here is that God is able to provide you with enough *to do the good things he has called you to do*, including giving to others who are in need. While people who misuse this Scripture today make people focus on getting more money for themselves, Paul's point is that Christians should not be concerned with getting God's blessing, but rather with being God's blessing to those in need around them.

Christians, of all people, can afford to be generous, according to Paul, not least because of how generous God is to us in Christ. But Christian generosity is undergirded by the added promises that God will provide for his people *precisely in order* that they might be generous.

By participating in this ministry of giving, the Corinthians are to demonstrate that they are a part of God's new community. The self-centred parochial concerns that each one brings to the table will be transformed. Giving will demonstrate their love, which will also bear witness to the reality of their new life in Christ.

There is another New Testament hint of what stewardship looked like (or didn't look like) in the early church. Paul, in his letter to the Christians in Philippi, commended them for supporting him financially as he engaged in further missionary work – even though other churches had not.

This tells us that stewardship did not come naturally to the first generation of Christians – just as it doesn't come naturally to Christians today. Paul condemned no one for this slowness. Nor was he seeking to get rich off the kindness of others. Instead he viewed his own needs in apostolic ministry as an opportunity for others to excel in the blessing of giving, promising that "my God will fully satisfy every need of yours according to his riches in glory in Christ Jesus" (Philippians 4:19).

Christian stewardship prompts Christians to be a channel of the blessings God has given us. Paul states that as we give of what God has given us, God will not only provide what we need but will entrust us with even more to give in his name. God doesn't satisfy our greedy desires or bankroll an extravagant lifestyle. But when we align ourselves with his priorities and give ourselves sacrificially for the sake of his kingdom, God will bless and enable us as his people to do what he calls us to do.

WHAT IS "PURE RELIGION"?

James, the first bishop of the Jerusalem church, provided further evidence of how closely Christian belief was tied to Christian behaviour in general and Christian charity in particular. In his characteristically blunt way, James simply said: "Religion that is pure and undefiled before God, the Father, is this: to care for orphans and widows in their distress, and to keep oneself unstained by the world" (James 1:27). When James brought up the issue of genuine faith as opposed to its counterfeit, he chose an example that has to do with the needy:

> What good is it, my brothers and sisters, if you say you have faith but do not have works? Can faith save you? If a brother or sister is naked and lacks daily food, and one of you says to them, 'Go in peace; keep warm and eat your fill', and yet you do not supply their bodily needs, what is the good of that? So faith by itself, if it has no works, is dead (James 2:14-17).

James makes our use of material possessions – our stewardship – a matter of our fundamental standing before God.

James makes our use of material possessions – our stewardship – a matter of our fundamental standing before God. In this case, works are what we choose to do with what we have. It would not be a stretch to say that, for James, faith without stewardship is dead.

When ideas about stewardship surface in the New Testament epistles, they emerge fully formed and with passion. Churches gave towards ongoing feeding for needy widows and orphans or one-time donations to feed distant congregations in famine. They supported their giving with leadership structures, developed fundraising campaigns, and delegated trustworthy individuals to follow up.

What we *don't* see in the New Testament is a church *not* thinking about money or stewardship. Instead, these early believers were fully engaged with supporting local ministers and ministries, and fully capable of responding to extraordinary needs as they arose. The evidence suggests that Jewish and Gentile churches treated the teachings of Jesus or the apostles on matters of money and stewardship as what they were expected to do too. The quick snapshots of the churches bear this out.

Later, when the number of Christians increased enough to be noticed, they acquired the reputation of taking care of the poor and needy. By the time their neighbours began to take Christians seriously, stewardship was their habit, the default position of individual Christians and local churches. We can now begin to see why. Eminent sociologist Rodney Stark explains that cities in the Greco-Roman world were miserable places, but Christian relationships gave new life to those cities:

> To cities filled with the homeless and impoverished, Christianity offered charity as well as hope. To cities filled with newcomers and strangers, Christianity offered an immediate basis for attachment. To cities filled with orphans and widows, Christianity provided a new and expanded sense of family. To cities torn by violent ethnic strife, Christianity offered a new basis for social solidarity . . . And to cities faced with epidemics, fires, and earthquakes, Christianity offered effective nursing services . . . For what they brought was not simply an urban movement, but a *new culture* capable of making life in Greco-Roman cities more tolerable.[19]

Of course, the early Christians had their issues and even scandals, like churches today. But the way they dealt with their money and resources was different enough from the surrounding cultures to attract attention, and most likely new converts as well.

THE HARVEST

It's sad how many Christians believe it's impossible to live like the early church. Our own unwillingness to change doesn't change whether the Scriptures themselves are true or God's call is valid! So we remain with our persistent poverty and corruption instead of the vision of a Christian community we see in Acts. When it comes to being God's blessing for our community, we are too often our own worst enemies.

This reminds us that, in our own strength, we cannot transform ourselves into good stewards. So what is our part in the journey to becoming good stewards? If it's not about our efforts but the Holy Spirit working in us, do we have any role to play?

This is actually where I see the language of sowing and reaping providing a helpful analogy. One of the most memorable Old Testament images is a prophecy of blessing for the exiled remnant of Judah returning from captivity in Babylon:

> May those who sow in tears
> reap with shouts of joy.
> Those who go out weeping,
> bearing the seed for sowing,
> shall come home with songs of joy,
> carrying their sheaves (Psalm 126:5-6).

The words are few, but sweet. For many societies in biblical times, the time of sowing was often a lean season. The previous year's harvest and supplies would have been running low, and there would be nothing to replace the dwindling food stocks. If the previous year's crop had gone poorly, your family and the whole community might be facing disaster. You might have had to take some of the precious remaining grain and commit it to the earth rather than use it for food. Hence the image of planting with tears.

But that is what brought the harvest with the great joy of sheaves of grain gathered into the storehouse. The whole community would have been relieved as they experienced God's provision.

Christians must believe that God keeps his promises to provide for his people.

Stewardship is like sowing. Christians must trust that God loves them. Christians must believe that God keeps his promises to provide for his people. Christians must choose to take Jesus seriously when he says, "Seek first his kingdom and his righteousness, and all these things will be given to you as well" (Matthew 6:33 NIV). Christians must determine that choosing the security of God's side and giving themselves completely to God's agenda is better by far than choosing to compromise and getting involved with the world's side.

In the reality of our lives, things may not look so black and white. We may face opposition or ridicule. It may appear that the world's side is winning. And it might feel as if God is far away, or absent altogether. This is not unlike when a farmer sows seed. Nothing happens. Days go by. But the experienced farmer knows that this is what happens with seeds. They get put into the earth, and they just sit there.

But science has shown us that seeds are undergoing an immense transformation on the inside, getting ready to explode the hard shell and take on an entirely new, different, and immensely productive life. When the seed is ready, all it usually takes is a little bit of rain, and then it explodes.

The farmer notices some tender green shoots poking up through the earth. He cannot see that, underneath, each seed is sending out a root to tap into the moisture and nourishment in the soil. What used to be a seed now becomes a factory, transforming water, minerals, and nutrients into roots, stems, and leaves, using the sun's power to produce food for the rapidly expanding number of cells that make up the growing plant.

This is similar to what happens when we human beings get rightly related to God through our repentance and forgiveness that comes to us through Christ's death on the cross. Jesus says, "Very truly, I tell you, unless a grain of wheat falls into the earth and dies, it remains just a single grain; but if it dies, it bears much fruit" (John 12:24). The call to stewardship is ultimately not a call to success, or to blessing, or to happiness. It is a call to die. There is a solution to the problem in our hearts and in our churches, but it will cost us everything we have. "I am the way," says Jesus. "Follow me," says Jesus. "If any want to become my followers, let them deny themselves and take up their cross and follow me" (Mark 8:34). This is the decision that everyone who wants to be a Christian must make. Jesus is asking us to surrender our self-centred lives and trust God, putting everything back into his hands for him to use for his glory.

The cost may seem too high. But when we consider the alternative, Jesus's way to life always wins out over our world's way to death. Jesus calls us not only to die to the calls of this world, but also to be raised to new life. A life that now belongs to God. A life that's free to follow Christ. A life that's free to be God's partner as he reclaims his world. A life that is free to become God's blessing to the church and to those around each of us.

The question simply is, am I willing to follow Jesus? Am I willing to trust Jesus? Am I willing to sacrifice everything that I am and everything that I have? Am I willing to do what he wants me to do? Am I willing to go where he wants me to go?

In our partnership with God, it's not a 50%-50% arrangement. Instead it's 100%-100%. We give everything *and* God does everything. It's the same principle Paul describes with respect to our salvation in his letter to the Philippian Christians: "Work out your salvation with fear and trembling; for it is God who is at work in you, enabling you both to will and to work for his good pleasure" (Philippians 2:12b-13). In stewardship, we give back to God what was already his to begin with. We give it all, because it is his, not ours. We give it for him to use for his glory, because he is the owner of it all, and we are simply managing what is his under his direction.

A CHURCH THAT REACHED OUT

Like the early church, our churches have a broader responsibility than taking care of our own members. Our resources are needed in service of a more radical vision to disciple all nations. I became familiar with a wealthy congregation in a university town who lived this out. It had started as a small group unhappy with their previous church, specifically with the corruption of their leaders and the complacency of their fellow church members.

The church attracted people with its biblical preaching and through the members' outreach to unchurched friends and neighbours. The church realized they would soon outgrow their location. The leadership made a radical decision. Many churches would have built a larger building to house their growing congregation. But this church decided to multiply their church by preparing 200 members over the course of a year to establish another congregation in a different part of the town or in a neighbouring community. They trained their leaders and sent out their members.

The first new church was an immediate success and began drawing in people from the surrounding neighbourhoods. The mother church was so encouraged by the results that they did this again and again. To date they have established six thriving congregations where hardly any meaningful Christian witness existed before.

Yes, the mother church missed their former members. They prayed regularly for God's blessing on the new congregations. But as they continued their own outreach and mercy ministries, they continued to grow. For over 20 years they have held to their original vision of multiplying their church, and they continue to be God's blessing in that city.

They may not look impressive compared to the megachurches nearby who have enormous buildings and crowds of well-dressed people flowing in every Sunday. But this college town church has a huge impact for the gospel. Instead of spending their resources on their own comfort and prestige, they have prioritized increasing the witness of Christ in their area. It all started because the members have taken seriously their call to be disciples and to participate in the advance of the Kingdom of God in their town. Their commitment to discipleship drives their vision, and their commitment to stewardship makes it happen.

Am I completely at the Lord's disposal for him to use for his glory?

This church's story encourages us. When we surrender what we have, we come alive, just like the seed buried in the ground. We glimpse the harvest with joy. The New Testament letters remind us that stewardship is never just about money, it's about transformation – the transformation of our lives as we become God's blessing in the lives of others, and the transformation of our churches into the very presence and power of Jesus in our communities. Christians can respond in many ways to the needs of those around them and beyond their circles. The fundamental issue is simply this: am I completely at the Lord's disposal for him to use for his glory? That's stewardship. That's God's goal for us as his born-again children. That's God's goal for us as his church.

BIBLE STUDY SEVEN

CARING FOR THE GLOBAL BODY

A bad famine had hit the eastern Mediterranean world. The Christians of Jerusalem and Judea had been badly affected. Paul organized an offering for the mother church from the Gentile churches he had helped to establish. He personally asked the church in Corinth to do their part. They willingly committed. As the time approached, Paul became anxious to travel to Jerusalem. He needed the Corinthians to follow through with their intentions. In this conversation, Paul reminds, persuades, and uses every tactic possible to urge the Christians of Corinth to fulfil their earlier pledge to help.

In this part of Paul's letter to the Corinthians, we learn a lot about reasons to be good stewards and reasons to share. The chief reason is the example of Jesus himself. Let's listen in.

2 Corinthians 8:1-15

1 We want you to know, brothers and sisters, about the grace of God
that has been granted to the churches of Macedonia; 2 for during a
severe ordeal of affliction, their abundant joy and their extreme
poverty have overflowed in a wealth of generosity on their part. 3 For,
as I can testify, they voluntarily gave according to their means, and
even beyond their means, 4 begging us earnestly for the privilege of
sharing in this ministry to the saints – 5 and this, not merely as we
expected; they gave themselves first to the Lord and, by the will of
God, to us, 6 so that we might urge Titus that, as he had already made
a beginning, so he should also complete this generous undertaking
among you. 7 Now as you excel in everything – in faith, in speech, in
knowledge, in utmost eagerness, and in our love for you – so we want
you to excel also in this generous undertaking.

8 I do not say this as a command, but I am testing the genuineness of
your love against the earnestness of others. 9 For you know the

generous act of our Lord Jesus Christ, that though he was rich, yet for your sakes he became poor, so that by his poverty you might become rich. [10] And in this matter I am giving my advice: it is appropriate for you who began last year not only to do something but even to desire to do something – [11] now finish doing it, so that your eagerness may be matched by completing it according to your means. [12] For if the eagerness is there, the gift is acceptable according to what one has – not according to what one does not have. [13] I do not mean that there should be relief for others and pressure on you, but it is a question of a fair balance between [14] your present abundance and their need, so that their abundance may be for your need, in order that there may be a fair balance. [15] As it is written,

'The one who had much did not have too much,
    and the one who had little did not have too little.'

Questions to Discuss

1. Paul holds up the churches of Macedonia as an example of Christian giving. What did they do that Paul thinks is exemplary?
2. Paul also holds up the example of Jesus himself as a model for Christian giving. How was Jesus "rich"? How did Jesus become "poor"?
3. How are the Corinthians to follow Jesus's example of self-giving? How about us today?
4. In verses 12-15, what principles does Paul recommend for Christian aid to other groups of Christians?
5. In verse 15, Paul quotes Exodus 16:18, which describes how God provided manna for his people to eat in the wilderness. In that passage, Israel learned that God would provide enough for everyone. Have you ever worried that you would not have enough if you also gave to help someone else?
6. Can you tell a story from the Bible or your own life of a time someone gave from the little they had and saw God provide? How does this affect your feelings of worry?

CHAPTER EIGHT

A GREAT CLOUD OF WITNESSES: PART ONE

What happened when those first apostles, who had heard Jesus's teaching on stewardship from his own mouth, departed this life? Did the first-century Christians begin to change with the passing of time?

Fortunately for us, many texts written by leaders and writers from the first millennium have survived. These documents give glimpses into the lives and priorities of their times. As we shall see, issues of money and stewardship were just as important to Christians and their churches then as they are now. We will also notice that the idea of stewardship in the early church was always about much more than just tithing. None of the writings that survive from the first 150 years of Christianity suggest either a monetary or percentage amount that Christians should give, but they show radical sacrifice and great concern for the poor. In chapter three, we quoted Irenaeus, the Bishop of Lyon at the end of the second century, describing Jesus's teaching in the Gospels and the practice of New Testament Christians:

> They [O.T. saints] offered their tithes; but those who have received liberty set apart everything they have for the Lord's use, cheerfully and freely giving them (2 Corinthians 9:7), not as small things in the hope of greater, but like that poor widow, who put her whole livelihood into the treasury of God (Luke 21:4).[20]

As we will see, in the first five centuries of the church, people really lived out these convictions. They called each new generation of Christians back to the same criterion of godliness regarding money and property: *Our very lives belong to God, and our calling as Christians is to make what he has given to us available for his use.*

How the church in centuries past understood their call to be stewards of their money and resources – the little that they had – made a tangible difference in the lives of their members and those around them. People around them took notice, and the church kept growing. Let's take a look at their example in the hopes that we too can make a similar difference in our world today.

THE DIDACHE

One of the earliest writings we have, called *The Teaching of the Twelve Apostles*, or the *Didache* (a Greek noun meaning "teaching"), is a kind of church manual. It was apparently written by an unknown member of that second generation of Christian writers we call the Apostolic Fathers, perhaps as early as the mid to late first century.[21] In one striking passage, it states:

> Do not be one who holds his hand out to take but shuts it when it comes to giving . . . for you will discover who [God] is that pays you back a reward with a good grace. Do not turn your back on the needy, but share everything with your brother and call nothing your own. For if you have what is eternal in common, how much more should you have what is transient! (*Didache* 4:5-8)

For if you have what is eternal in common, how much more should you have what is transient!

This paragraph echoes what the early Jerusalem church did in Acts 2 and 4, who knew that if they already shared things that will last forever, they should certainly be willing to share the things on earth.

Christian generosity and hospitality give evidence of one's salvation, but they are not to be abused. Apparently, early Christians encountered many travellers claiming to be this or that person of importance in the church. Christians are to be generous, the *Didache* says, but not gullible:

> Welcome every apostle on arriving, as if he were the Lord. But he must not stay beyond one day. In case of necessity, however, the next day too. If he stays three days, he is a false prophet. On departing, an apostle must not accept anything save sufficient food to carry him till his next lodging. If he asks for money, he is a false prophet (*Didache* 11:3-6).

The next chapter gives the same guidelines for other Christian visitors travelling through. After three days, the guest must work for his living in a trade or help the host in other ways. *Didache* 12:1-5 warns: "If he refuses to do this, he is trading on Christ. You must be on your guard against such people." The fact that the author speaks against these things tells us that such abusers of Christian generosity were somewhat common.

Today we see many claiming to be men or women of God. Perhaps they come to your village and expect to be hosted. They begin having services and extracting offerings. But too often there is no accountability. Too often their titles are self-generated.

There are legitimate evangelists and pastors called by God into a sacrificial ministry amongst God's people. Welcoming them and supporting their ministry is an act of service to God and to the church. But some people today, just as during the time of the *Didache,* are in it for the money and taking advantage of Christians. We should be cautious of people who expect others to support them and use spiritual threats if anyone challenges their authority. If we followed the *Didache's* advice and removed money from the equation, I wonder how many of these so-called apostles, prophets, and servants of God would stay around?

CLEMENT OF ALEXANDRIA

Clement of Alexandria (AD 150-215) was an African convert to Christianity. He taught at the Catechetical School in Alexandria and influenced a long line of remarkable leaders from the church in Egypt.

Alexandria was the second city of the Roman Empire, and the emperor Hadrian declared that the Alexandrians were "mutinous, empty-headed and troublesome; their city is rich, wealthy and prosperous; everyone is busy; their only god is money."[22]

In this context, Clement wrote a small treatise, *Can a Rich Man Be Saved?* Clement believed a rich man can in fact be saved, but he explained further how Christians should use money. He explained what Jesus meant in his Sermon on the Mount when he said: "Blessed are the poor in spirit, for theirs is the kingdom of heaven" (Matthew 5:3 NRSV-A). People who are "poor in spirit" see their possessions as gifts God has given them to save others and for the sake of others. Their focus is on doing good work, so they will be equally cheerful if they lose their possessions.[23] But the rich person who cannot be saved is the one who "carries his riches in his soul, and instead of God's Spirit bears in his heart gold or land." His focus is on always getting more possessions on earth, so he can't possibly focus on the kingdom of heaven. "For where the mind of a man is, there is also his treasure," Clement paraphrases.[24]

How much of your mind do you devote to money, and how much time do you spend thinking about serving God and others?

Our culture's view of money may not be very different from Alexandria's long ago. Are your peers absorbed by trying to get ahead, making investments, and buying luxury items? Does your family or your community pressure you to be successful by your culture's definition? Clement is an excellent example of a Christian leader who didn't give in to pressure. Despite living in a city where everyone's god was money, Clement refused to follow his culture's expectations. He challenged Christians under his leadership to live by a different set of values. He observed that riches were generally toxic to the faith handed down from the apostles. The only escape was to use one's riches in a *Christian* way, meeting the needs of others with the plenty of what one has. Take his challenge to heart and consider: how much of your mind do you devote to money, and how much time do you spend thinking about serving God and others?

MARCUS MINUCIUS FELIX

The early Christians were a mostly poor, sometimes persecuted minority. But the way they lived caught the attention of their neighbours. Some pagans viewed Christian poverty as a sign of weakness or even wickedness. A Christian named Marcus Minucius Felix (died circa AD 250 in Rome)[25] responded that Christians should be admired, not shamed, for their poverty, because it strengthened their character. The truly poor, in his view, were those who always felt they didn't have enough possessions. But Christians without material possessions were not poor, because they were content with what they had, including having God's presence. Marcus said: "When a man walks along a road, the lighter he travels, the happier he is; equally, on this journey of life, a man is more blessed if he does not pant beneath a burden of riches but lightens his load by poverty."

He said if Christians needed anything, they could ask the God who owns everything, but he believed what Christians really wanted to ask God for was innocence, patience, and goodness.[26]

Most Christians on the continent of Africa are poor. Some so-called Christian prophets and apostles would like to make us feel ashamed of our poverty when we see their lavish lifestyles, fancy cars and houses, and even private jets. Successful but corrupt businessmen or politicians may also look down on us Christians who are poor because we refuse to cheat others. Sometimes we may even wonder if we are cursed. But really the people who are becoming wealthy unjustly are the ones bringing judgement on themselves. Although it is an unpopular opinion, Marcus reminds us that we can be grateful that we have few possessions, finding our contentment in God as he grows our character.

CYPRIAN OF CARTHAGE

The African bishop Cyprian of Carthage (in modern day Tunisia) reflected on the causes behind the defection of so many Christians during the persecutions of mid-third century North Africa. Cyprian said many had lost their first love for Christ. Instead, they had become passionate about acquiring more and more wealth. "Gone was the devotion of bishops to the service of God, gone was the clergy's faithful integrity, gone the generous compassion for the needy, gone all discipline in our behaviour." He specifically pointed out:

> Too many bishops, instead of giving encouragement and example to others, [ignored the ministry] which God had entrusted to them, and took up the administration of secular business: they . . . abandoned their people, and toured the markets in other territories on the look-out for profitable deals. If that is what we have become, what do we not deserve for such sins?[27]

Does this sound like some of the bishops, pastors, priests, prophets, and apostles who have set up shop in churches and "ministries" all across our continent? There is a huge office and shopping building recently constructed on one of the main roads in Nairobi called the "Bishop M— Building". The man has certainly made a name for himself. But has he glorified God's name? If we have their words and actions to guide us, these false teachers seem much more concerned to make money for themselves and for their schemes than to be genuine disciples of Christ. If these are our shepherds, where will they lead the sheep?

RADICAL THEN, RADICAL NOW

When we hear about the false teachers in the days of the *Didache*, the wealth-obsessed Alexandrians, and the money-loving bishops, we remember that not all Christians in church history were exemplary in the use of their resources. There were rich Christians who tried to have it both ways, with one foot in the world of privilege and the other in the Kingdom of God. The fact that there are sermons and treatises on stewardship that have survived from this time period indicates that preachers, writers, and leaders saw stewardship as a major ongoing issue they always needed to address.

However, they also encourage us that the challenges people faced in the early years of Christianity are many of the same challenges we face today. How convicting then to realize that despite these same pressures, ordinary Christians in the past generously shared what they had. The record tells again and again in church history that men and women converted to Christianity and then chose to give away all of their possessions to the poor before moving into the wilderness or into a monastery in order to pray and become more like Christ. Because of the generosity of Christians, the number of poor people in various communities reduced so much so that it drew the mocking attention of the pagan elite, who cared nothing about such things. In a society opposed to the gospel, these Christians did not view the gospel teachings on money and stewardship as mere words. They took Jesus's commands about stewardship seriously. They believed that Christ's love obligated them to love one another even as he had loved them. And they left a lasting mark that we still read about centuries later.

BIBLE STUDY EIGHT

A GREAT CLOUD OF WITNESSES: PART ONE

Just as the church in Acts continued to preach and practise Jesus's radical money manifesto after he ascended to heaven, the church in the following century faithfully brought Christians back to the message of Jesus and the apostles. Sermons and treatises on stewardship that have survived from this time period indicate that preachers, writers, and leaders saw stewardship as a major ongoing issue they always needed to address. One of these was the small treatise, *Can a Rich Man Be Saved?* written by Clement of Alexandria (AD 150-215). Clement was an African convert to Christianity. He taught at the Catechetical School in Alexandria and influenced a long line of remarkable leaders from the church in Egypt. Alexandria was the second city of the Roman Empire, known for being wealthy, busy, and idolizing money. His context was not too different from our own, and his message still challenges us today.

Clement of Alexandria's treatise *Can a Rich Man Be Saved?* was based on Mark 10:17-31. Read the Bible passage and reflect with Clement on its meaning.

Mark 10:17-31

17 As [Jesus] was setting out on a journey, a man ran up and knelt
before him, and asked him, 'Good Teacher, what must I do to inherit
eternal life?' 18 Jesus said to him, 'Why do you call me good? No one is
good but God alone. 19 You know the commandments: "You shall not
murder; You shall not commit adultery; You shall not steal; You shall
not bear false witness; You shall not defraud; Honour your father and
mother."' 20 He said to him, 'Teacher, I have kept all these since my
youth.' 21 Jesus, looking at him, loved him and said, 'You lack one thing;
go, sell what you own, and give the money to the poor, and you will
have treasure in heaven; then come, follow me.' 22 When he heard this,
he was shocked and went away grieving, for he had many possessions.

23 Then Jesus looked around and said to his disciples, 'How hard it will
be for those who have wealth to enter the kingdom of God!' 24 And the
disciples were perplexed at these words. But Jesus said to them again,
'Children, how hard it is to enter the kingdom of God! 25 It is easier for
a camel to go through the eye of a needle than for someone who is
rich to enter the kingdom of God.' 26 They were greatly astounded and
said to one another, 'Then who can be saved?' 27 Jesus looked at them
and said, 'For mortals it is impossible, but not for God; for God all
things are possible.'

28 Peter began to say to him, 'Look, we have left everything and followed
you.' 29 Jesus said, 'Truly I tell you, there is no one who has left house or
brothers or sisters or mother or father or children or fields, for my sake
and for the sake of the good news, 30 who will not receive a hundredfold
now in this age – houses, brothers and sisters, mothers and children,
and fields, with persecutions – and in the age to come eternal life.
31 But many who are first will be last, and the last will be first.'

Questions to Discuss

1. What did the rich man say he wanted to obtain? What did his response reveal about what he really valued?
2. What does Jesus ask the rich man to do with his possessions? According to verses 29-31, what is a worthy motive for giving up one's possessions or relationships? How are these connected?
3. How does Jesus's challenge to the rich man compare to when Jesus called Peter (see Mark 1:16-18)? In that passage and this one, what rewards and difficulties are promised to people who sacrifice to follow Jesus?
4. Clement points out that having no property is not the key to eternal life, otherwise the best Christians would be beggars and pagans who gave up wealth to feel proud of themselves. Instead Jesus's challenge – which seemed impossible to both the rich man and Peter – was not to give up possessions, but to give up the passions of the soul such as the love of money and worry about money. The attitude that pleases God is unconcerned, Clement says: "If one has money, it is for the sake of his brethren;

if he does not have money, he is as cheerful as if he had. That is what it means to be poor in spirit."[28] Why do you think this is only possible with God?

5. Clement encourages eager giving: "Do not wait for Christians in need to ask you for help. Seek them out! As eagerly as a merchant looks for a new market, so should you seek out the needy. And do not ask which Christian is worthy and which is not. You may be wrong in your judgment and thereby deprive someone who needs your help. It is better to take the risk of giving to the undeserving than to take the risk of neglecting the deserving."[29] How can you seek out and give to a needy Christian this week?

CHAPTER NINE

A GREAT CLOUD OF WITNESSES: PART TWO

During the lifetime of the apostles, Christianity transitioned from being a small sect within Judaism to a religion that welcomed non-Jews throughout the Roman Empire and beyond. Over the next couple centuries, more and more people converted to Christianity. In several waves of persecution, the Roman government killed many Christians who refused to denounce their faith and worship the emperor. Then, Roman Emperor Constantine officially granted Christianity status as an acceptable religion in a law called the Edict of Milan (AD 313). The bloody years of state-sponsored persecution ended.

New and more subtle threats to the faith began to appear. When it became clear that Constantine himself may actually have become a Christian, joining a church began to be seen as a way of upward mobility, increasing one's chance for a good government job. Christianity became popular and churches were flooded with people who called themselves "Christians" but not all were true followers of Jesus.

As many wealthy, powerful, and worldly people joined the church, more seriously minded Christians fled into the desert to get away from worldly corruption. They wanted to pursue fundamental Christian spirituality. The monastic movement eventually became the source of much spiritual formation, missions, scholarship, and leadership. From the very beginning, the monks and nuns of Egypt, Palestine, and Syria emphasized the necessity of both poverty and charity.

Their poverty prophetically called people to repent from loving power and wealth.

There are many stories of the early desert fathers and mothers (monks and nuns) responding to God's call on their lives by giving away their possessions to the poor and simply trusting God to provide. I have already told the account of Anthony (in chapter five). The monks' life of simplicity could not have contrasted more with the over-the-top displays of wealth and power in the city churches. Their poverty prophetically called people to repent from loving power and wealth.

City-dwelling Christians began to seek out these monks of the desert as spiritual guides. Some of this was a kind of religious tourism; other people had more legitimate motives. Many of the desert fathers began to feel they were too close to town and it was too easy to find them. So they moved to even more remote locations.

Monasticism continued to spread into Asia Minor, Italy, and Gaul, then onward into Ireland and Britain. Today, there is still a huge monastic movement in Ethiopia amongst members of the Ethiopian Orthodox church, which is the oldest and longest surviving Christian church in sub-Saharan Africa. There are communities of monks and nuns scattered in almost every African country – Roman Catholic, Orthodox, and even Anglican – who have left material possessions in order to be free to do their ministries of charity and teaching.

BASIL OF CAESAREA

As the monastic movement was expanding in the fourth century, monks were increasingly seen as appropriate candidates to become bishops. In some cases, of course, the perks and power of these positions could erode their character and morality. But in other cases, the men selected as bishop of a particular area, town, or city saw the churches there respond with true renewal and even revival.

One such bishop was Basil of Caesarea (circa AD 330-379). He preached a sermon about Christian stewardship probably in 368 when Asia Minor (Turkey) was experiencing a severe drought and shortage of food. Some of the rich were holding back grain in order to force the prices even higher. It reminds me of when there was a shortage of maize flour in Kenya, and some mills were withholding the flour they had to try and get a better price.

In Basil's congregation, there were suffering men, women, and children, as well as people who had plenty and were doing nothing to help those in desperate need, Basil was justifiably angry. He preached: "'Who am I injuring,' you will say, 'when I keep what is mine for myself?' And what, tell me, is yours? And from where have you brought it with you into this life?" God has given resources to you and not to others, Basil argued, it is not because God is unjust, but because he is giving you an opportunity to earn rewards for being compassionate, patient, and stewarding your resources well.[30]

"If each took only what was sufficient for his needs, and left what remained, there would be no rich and no poor," Basil pointed out.[31] If you are not content with enough and you keep more than you need when others need it, Basil says you will be judged:

> That bread you hold in your clutches, that belongs to the starving. That cloak you keep locked away in your wardrobe, that belongs to the naked. Those shoes that are going to waste with you, they belong to the barefooted. That silver you buried away, that belongs to the needy. Whomsoever you could have helped and did not, to so many you have been unjust.[32]

In a previous chapter, we mentioned how the Hebrew word for giving alms (*zedekah)* also meant righteousness, because it was only giving the poor what belonged to them. Basil's words may sound strong, but they are very biblical.

I am surrounded by people who have much less than I have. I cannot open my closet and look at my many pairs of shoes without thinking of what Bishop Basil said to the wealthy members of his church. Nor can I look into my cupboard with all my choices of things to eat without thinking of those who have nothing. What about you? What things do you have more than enough of? Who in your community might need some of these things that God has put in your care to distribute?

AMBROSE

Meanwhile in the Western part of the Roman Empire, Ambrose (circa AD 340-397) was the son of a high-ranking political figure. He had been brought up in a Christian family and had risen to prominence as a gifted civil administrator and governor of Milan.

Then the bishop of Milan died. This led to a spasm of civil strife, during which the people fixed on Ambrose to be their bishop, even though he wasn't even a priest. After going into hiding, he sensed God's call and allowed himself to be ordained.

He gave his possessions to the poor, donated his land to the church, and entrusted his family into the care of his brother.

As a bishop, Ambrose immediately adopted the simple lifestyle of an ascetic. After ensuring a living for his sister, he gave his possessions to the poor, donated his land to the church, and entrusted his family into the care of his brother. Because of these personal choices, Ambrose was viewed as a man who spoke with integrity and whose life matched his rhetoric.

As with Basil in the East, Ambrose repeatedly clashed with Christians in his diocese who felt they could have it all, both worldly treasure and spiritual security. In his sermon on 1 Kings 21 (circa AD 395), Ambrose explained that the earth was made for everyone, so how can rich people claim exclusive rights to the soil? From nature's perspective, we are naked when we are born and when we die.[33] Therefore, he found the difference between rich and poor unjust: "The people are starving, and you close your barns; the people weep bitterly, and you toy with a jewelled ring . . . The jewel in your ring could preserve the lives of the whole people."

According to Ambrose, someone who was unable to give their inheritance to the poor showed that they were a servant to their wealth instead of mastering it. In such a case, "the man belongs to his riches, not the riches to the man."[34]

Inheritance is very important in many of cultures in Africa. In some cases, families can be divided and stop speaking for years because of conflicts over inheritance. But when we see the example of Ambrose, we see that he was more concerned with his eternal security than his financial security. Could you donate your inherited land to the church? Could you give up a prominent government post to serve God's people? As Christian leaders today, the power of our message will be most visible in the way it is changing our own lives. Do we show by the way we live that following Christ is worth *everything?*

AUGUSTINE

Ambrose's reputation as a preacher with spiritual integrity drew a North African seeker on the fringes of Christianity into his congregation. Augustine (AD 354-430) had dabbled in different religious beliefs and become sceptical. He had moved from Carthage to Rome and then to Milan, where he had been given a prestigious position teaching rhetoric.

Augustine was attracted to Bishop Ambrose's rhetorical skills. Soon Augustine began to take seriously what the bishop was preaching. Eventually, Augustine embraced Christianity.

Shortly before his conversion, Augustine had been reading about the life of Anthony the desert father. He was already acquainted with the lifestyle choices of his spiritual patron Ambrose. So, it is not surprising that Augustine himself chose to adopt the simple life of a monk when he finally moved back to the North African town of Hippo. He became a bishop there and is still remembered as one of the greatest leaders of the early church.

In the West today, many consider eschewing private possessions to be a kind of Marxist heresy, but among the early Christians it was viewed as the way to follow Christ and to gain an eternal inheritance in the life to come. Augustine argued that lawsuits, quarrels, and even murder come from our private property ownership. He said: "What are we fighting over? Over the things we call our own. We do not go to law about things we possess in common, do we? We all breathe in the air that belongs to all of us, and we all enjoy the sunshine that is common to all."

Augustine said Christians should focus on making a place for the Lord to dwell, so we must avoid becoming attached to private possessions, which will distract us from loving Christ.[35] He contrasted genuine Christian spirituality with materialism. Anything that shuts the door in Christ's face must be avoided at all costs; he observed that material possessions and property often do just that. If that is radical to our ears, it is because of the materialistic culture we live in, not because it isn't in the Bible. In the Gospels themselves, Jesus said pointedly that one cannot serve both God and earthly wealth. New Testament Christianity, as well as the Christianity of the early church, viewed divestment of one's possessions as one of the great fruits of genuine Christian spirituality.

There were, of course, the practical benefits to sharing property – the poor in one's community were cared for, and legitimate needs could be addressed. But the main point that emerges again and again is that believing one's possessions belong completely to God and using them accordingly is simply good for one's soul. Life is about more than possessions, and we cannot enter into the life of Christ whilst dragging a pile of earthly goods.

In my part of Africa, land ownership is the goal of acquiring wealth. Land is valuable capital in countries with growing populations and often produces returns even in uncertain economies, similar to how people in the West view the stock market. Unfortunately, we have a huge problem with land-grabbing, that is, using bribes to alter official records so that your land is now actually mine. So much cultural pressure is put upon us to get land that many do not see how this form of materialism corrodes our hearts. People regularly choose to be something other than Christian when it comes to getting and holding on to land. But what good is it, Jesus asks us, if we gain the whole world (and all its land) but forfeit our soul? (Matthew 16:26). What Augustine taught, indeed what Christ taught, cuts across our cultures with regard to land, stocks, possessions, and wealth.

JOHN CHRYSOSTOM

The last of the early church leaders we will consider in this survey is John Chrysostom (circa AD 349-407), Bishop of Constantinople. (*Chrysostom* means 'golden-mouthed' in view of his eloquent, powerful, biblical preaching.) John is yet another example of a Christian who abandoned his wealth and property for the sake of obeying Christ. His commitment to self-inflicted poverty infused his preaching and produced powerful calls for his hearers to follow the example of Christ and the apostles in their own lives.

"Our money is the Lord's, however we may have gathered it."

In one sermon on the Rich Man and Lazarus (Luke 16:19-31), John pointed out that the rich man was tortured after death, seemingly judged like a thief even though he did not take anything from Lazarus, but simply because he did not share with him.[36] John quoted other Scriptures to make his point that "when we do not show mercy, we will be punished just like those who steal. For our money is the Lord's, however we may have gathered it."[37] Indeed, this last sentence is the principle at the heart of both Christian stewardship and Christian charity: what we have is not our own, but given for us to use.

John powerfully communicated the teaching of the Scriptures. He felt he was merely passing on to his hearers, not what they wanted to hear, but what the Word of God was actually saying:

> God has allowed you to have more: not for you to waste on prostitutes, drink, fancy food, expensive clothes, and all the other kinds of indolence, but for you to distribute to those in need. Just as an official in the imperial treasury, if he neglects to distribute where he is ordered, but spends instead for his own indolence, pays the penalty and is put to death, so also the rich man is a kind of steward of the money which is owed for distribution to the poor. He is directed to distribute it to his fellow servants who are in want. So, if he spends more on himself than his need requires, he will pay the harshest penalty hereafter. For his own goods are not his own but belong to his fellow servants.[38]

Statements like these got him into trouble with the empress in Constantinople and with a clique of wealthy and powerful people there, and ultimately cost him his life. But the church recognized that John's preaching reflected the heart of Christianity and the gospel. Nothing could be more radical in the ears of those who felt they had too much treasure and property to lose. But nothing could be more instructive in the ears of one who took seriously the call of Christ to "deny himself, take up his cross and follow me" (Mark 8:34 NRSV-A).

BLESSED TO BLESS OTHERS

The surprising lesson about money and Christians, expounded again and again by leaders from the first five centuries of Christian history, is that for the Christian, all money is God's money. Today, we debate a lot about offerings and tithes and stewardship, whether a Christian is obligated or not to give to the church, and if so, how much. But for the first 500 years of the church, people were practising this, not just talking about it. We have a lot to learn from the words and example of these early brothers and sisters in Christ.

If what you have is God's property to give to others, you might ask: "Is there any blessing for me along the way?" Yes, of course. But not in the usual understanding of that word. All over the African countries where I have lived or visited, churchgoers are running after blessing. Everyone wants to be blessed. For many, this means financial prosperity, the ability to do whatever they want, to have whatever they want, to go wherever they want, to be whatever they want to be. In earlier times here on the

African continent, blessing meant that my family and I were free from illness, that I had many children, that my sheep and goats and cattle were increasing in number, that my crops produced abundantly and there was no drought or famine, and that we were protected from curses. This certainly is an aspect of blessing in the Bible.

But the most important part is missing. In the Old and New Testaments, blessing doesn't come solely to be consumed by the blessed. As we heard in the excerpts and testimonies of the Church Fathers in this chapter, when you or I receive blessing, we are then enabled to be God's blessing to those around us. This involves taking care of each other and also spreading God's blessing to people different from us. We are blessed to bless, as the Lord said to Abraham in Genesis 12:1-3:

> 'Go from your country and your kindred and your father's house to the land that I will show you. I will make of you a great nation, and I will bless you, and make your name great, so that you will be a blessing. I will bless those who bless you, and the one who curses you I will curse; and in you all the families of the earth shall be blessed'.

This is the essence of stewardship, both in the Old Testament and the New. This is God's desire for us as his church. The world has always been eager for the blessing part. Many counterfeit versions of Christianity have pretended to have found the secret of unlocking God's blessing and prosperity for your life. But we are blessed to bless, not to be selfishly prosperous, as if prosperity were somehow a sign of God's favour, and not being prosperous a sign of God's curse. The apostle Paul, in his farewell message to the Ephesian elders, uses his own work as an example of giving everything one has in service of others:

> 'I coveted no one's silver or gold or clothing. You know for yourselves that I worked with my own hands to support myself and my companions. In all this I have given you an example that by such work we must support the weak, remembering the words of the Lord Jesus, for he himself said, "It is more blessed to give than to receive"' (Acts 20:33-35).

Christian stewardship is moving in a fundamentally different direction from the world's rush after blessing. We must be careful that Christian stewardship does not sink down into mere self-centredness. Like Ananias and Sapphira, we may think we can easily give a portion to God and hold on to the rest for ourselves (Acts 5:1-11). Through our giving and our prayers, we may try to manipulate God to get what we want. We can easily act like Jesus's disciples before they understood what Jesus was teaching, trying to force Jesus into our own presuppositions and expectations about money, leadership, spirituality, or the purpose of his kingdom (Mark 10:35-45).

Christian stewardship is moving in a fundamentally different direction from the world's rush after blessing.

When our mindset shifts to being stewards, we are no longer concerned about how much or how little we have. We realize that everything we are and have belongs to God. We give thanks that God has blessed us and entrusted us with these gifts. Our lives consist of managing what God has given in ways that help us to love God with all our heart and enable us to love our neighbour. It's not about being blessed but passing on God's blessing to others. Stewardship is that simple – and that challenging.

God's call to be stewards is so different from the world's understanding that it requires a complete mindset shift. It isn't just that all money is God's money. It's that our whole lives belong to God. As modern Christians influenced by the West (including by Western missionaries), we often put money in its own special category. But the leaders of the early Christians did not isolate different components like stewardship or discipleship or one's prayer life or participation in the life of a church, as if one could do one and not the others. Just as without prayer, one could question whether one was genuinely a Christian, without stewardship we should ask the same question. A Christian, a follower of Jesus, by definition will be a steward of all the things God has entrusted to her or him.[39] Where this is not happening, it is reasonable to suspect that something is defective in one's Christian life. A good tree will produce good fruit. Whether long ago or in our own day, we know God is at work when we see Christians giving sacrificially and cheerfully for the sake of the poor, for the sake of the church, and to advance the gospel of the Kingdom of God.

A GREAT CLOUD OF WITNESSES: PART TWO

Two leaders of the church in its first few centuries were Bishop Basil of Caesarea (circa AD 330-379), who ministered in Asia Minor (Turkey), and the Bishop of Constantinople, John Chrysostom (circa AD 349-407). Both of these men gave away their property to follow Christ and preached a radical money manifesto that they believed was consistent with the teachings of Jesus. Their teachings and lifestyles challenged both their original hearers and us today.

Let's read a well-known stewardship parable Jesus told, alongside some insights from these Church Fathers.

Matthew 25:14-30

> [14] 'For it is as if a man, going on a journey, summoned his slaves and
> entrusted his property to them; [15] to one he gave five talents, to another
> two, to another one, to each according to his ability. Then he went
> away. [16] The one who had received the five talents went off at once and
> traded with them, and made five more talents. [17] In the same way, the
> one who had the two talents made two more talents. [18] But the one
> who had received the one talent went off and dug a hole in the ground
> and hid his master's money. [19] After a long time the master of those
> slaves came and settled accounts with them. [20] Then the one who had
> received the five talents came forward, bringing five more talents,
> saying, "Master, you handed over to me five talents; see, I have made
> five more talents." [21] His master said to him, "Well done, good and
> trustworthy slave; you have been trustworthy in a few things, I will put
> you in charge of many things; enter into the joy of your master." [22] And
> the one with the two talents also came forward, saying, "Master, you
> handed over to me two talents; see, I have made two more talents."
> [23] His master said to him, "Well done, good and trustworthy slave; you
> have been trustworthy in a few things, I will put you in charge of many

things; enter into the joy of your master." 24 Then the one who had
received the one talent also came forward, saying, "Master, I knew that
you were a harsh man, reaping where you did not sow, and gathering
where you did not scatter seed; 25 so I was afraid, and I went and hid
your talent in the ground. Here you have what is yours." 26 But his master
replied, "You wicked and lazy slave! You knew, did you, that I reap
where I did not sow, and gather where I did not scatter? 27 Then you
ought to have invested my money with the bankers, and on my return
I would have received what was my own with interest. 28 So take the
talent from him, and give it to the one with the ten talents. 29 For to all
those who have, more will be given, and they will have an abundance;
but from those who have nothing, even what they have will be taken
away. 30 As for this worthless slave, throw him into the outer darkness,
where there will be weeping and gnashing of teeth."'

Questions to Discuss

1. Church Father John Chrysostom said, "God has invested capital with you. It is not your property, but a loan by him, made to give you opportunity to exercise mercy on those who are in need."[40] If the investing in this parable referred to giving to the poor, how would it affect your reaction to the parable?
2. In the passage that immediately follows this, Matthew describes Jesus separating people at the final judgement like sheep from goats (see Bible Study Four). What similarities or connections do you see between the two parables?
3. Basil of Caesarea said, "Are you not a robber? You who treat as absolutely yours what you received that you might dispense to others[?] He who strips another man of his clothing, is he not called a robber; and he who does not clothe the naked when he could, should he not be called the same?"[41] What do you think of Basil's comment in light of these two parables?
4. What is the third servant's view of the master? How does this affect his use of resources?
5. How do you think your view of God affects how you use your resources?

6. In order to use their master's money well, the servants needed to know their master's goals for his resources. This book has defined stewardship as using God's resources for his purposes. From what we have studied in this book, what are some of God's purposes for using the money he has entrusted to you?

CHAPTER TEN

RECLAIMING REAL STEWARDSHIP

If stewardship involves leaving behind everything our world has told us about blessing and totally changing our mindsets, it's clearly not a programme we can accomplish with a few quick steps. Becoming a steward may seem completely impossible! And if we had to transform ourselves with our own strength, it would be.

It is hard for us to become stewards by trying to paint over our old life with a new coat of Christian ideas, language, practices, and postures. We can't just change the outside. We need an inner transformation. Becoming stewards requires beginning a new life, starting with Christ as the foundation for everything God wishes to do in and through us. This is why stewardship and discipleship are so closely related. In fact, from God's perspective, they may even be the same thing.

Jesus gives us this fresh start when we are born again (John 3:3 NIV). Jesus has died for us, and our old lives have died with him. So now we live our new lives for him: "He died for all, so that those who live might live no longer for themselves, but for him who died and was raised for them" (2 Corinthians 5:15). Our old selfish mindsets and values are gone. "So if anyone is in Christ, there is a new creation: everything old has passed away; see, everything has become new!" (2 Corinthians 5:17). Jesus promised to give his followers the Holy Spirit to enable them to follow him.

The biggest miracle that the Holy Spirit has been sent to accomplish is to transform us and make you and me more like Jesus.

I owe my early Christian experience to the charismatic movement. But I have lived long enough to realize that the biggest miracle that the Holy Spirit works in someone's life is not speaking in tongues or prophecy or healing; rather the biggest miracle that the Holy Spirit has been sent to accomplish is to transform us and make you and me more like Jesus. On the last day, Jesus won't care what miracles we worked or how many demons we may have cast out or whether or not we speak in tongues. He does care passionately about whether we have become like him and have been concerned to give our lives to do his Father's will (Matthew 7:21-23).

When God's Spirit is present and working in our hearts, he gives us a hunger and thirst for God's Word. As we read the Bible and hear God's teaching, we realize these are not just words and stories on a page, but they are applied by his Spirit to our lives and circumstances. We become eager to listen to preaching or teaching. We want to know what the Word says and what it means.

With understanding comes conviction. We realize we need to change. God begins to reorient our priorities around his. Every repentant, born-again, Spirit-filled disciple and steward of Christ becomes a life-changing invader on behalf of God's kingdom, or God's new creation in this fallen world.

So for the genuine Christian, stewardship, like discipleship, comes naturally, naturally in the sense that this is what the Holy Spirit *wants and intends* to work in us. It's not a change we have to create in ourselves, like trying to swim upstream. It is where the river of the Holy Spirit is carrying the small boat of our faith, and the ship of our church.

TRANSFORMED TO TRANSFORM

This same transformation happened to Jesus's first followers. They put off their old lives and were born again as new creations. They received the Holy Spirit. The change within them changed the world forever. And it was reflected in the way they practised stewardship. Take a look at this description of the church in Jerusalem in its early days:

> Now the whole group of those who believed were of one heart and soul; and no one claimed private ownership of any possessions, but everything they owned was held in common. With great power the apostles gave testimony to the resurrection of the Lord Jesus, and great grace was upon them all. There was not a needy person among them, for as many as owned lands or houses sold them and brought the proceeds of what was sold. They laid it at the apostles' feet, and it was distributed to each as any had need (Acts 4:32-35).

The early churches took Jesus's word seriously. They became known because of their stewardship and care for the poor. Their testimonies remain after all these years for anybody to read.

It's easy for us to find excuses for why we can't follow Jesus the way that the early church did. Many people in our churches may not know where their next meal will come from. When they pray in the Lord's Prayer for our Father to "give us this day our daily bread" it is for them not an empty phrase. It's easy to pass off this responsibility to some wealthier persons among us or outside donors. But let's compare ourselves to these early Christians for a moment.

The early Christians of the first, second, and third centuries had their issues, such as constantly struggling with false teachers. But they had none of the advantages that we have as Christians in most of Africa. In many countries, we have freedom of worship; they were periodically persecuted because it was illegal and considered subversive to be a Christian. We have TV, radio, internet, smartphones, and print publishing to help us get our message out; they had hand-delivered letters. We have vehicles, roads, and air travel. Their transport was by foot or using animals, and travel by sea was fraught with danger. If we consider ourselves to be relatively poor, or from poor, under-resourced countries, these people were, for the most part, poorer than we are, with no access to medical care, subject to the whims of weather and disease.

And yet, the Christian churches of the first three centuries grew and expanded so much that even empire-wide persecutions could not stop them. By the time Constantine became emperor in the fourth century, Christians were in the majority in many places, and paganism was in serious decline.

They took Jesus's radical call to be stewards and disciples seriously.

Why did the early church triumph? There are many factors feeding into a full answer to this question here. But at the top of the list is simply that they took Jesus's radical call to be stewards and disciples seriously. They were not, for the most part, interested in monetary gain or counting congregants. They weren't following Jesus because Christianity was popular, or a place where rich and powerful people could be found. They were following Jesus because they had come to know him and knowing him was changing everything for them. It's these simple people, responding to the call to be disciples and stewards, who God used to change the Roman world.

We might ask ourselves, what has changed between then and now? Has the fact that the church exists in a hostile, unfriendly environment changed between then and now? Has the gospel changed since the apostle Paul was making tents, writing letters, and being persecuted in every town? Not at all.

In fact, throughout this book we have looked at stewardship from the Old Testament through to the early church. We have opened our Bibles and seen for ourselves that stewardship and discipleship are at the heart of Jesus's teaching. We have seen God's people responding to his call right up into our present day on our own continent. God is still calling us to follow him, to give everything we have and are for his glory.

Becoming a Christian is responding to Jesus's call to follow him as his disciple. Discipleship means stewardship, and both mean a transformation of one's life, priorities, and direction. When we respond to Christ's call to be his steward and his disciple, we follow him down a very different path than the easy Christianity that is currently trending in our churches. Our churches begin to make a difference in their communities. Our churches become communities of disciples and stewards, who with their gifts and service become the body of Christ where they are – the presence of Jesus in our communities.

WE CAN BE STEWARDS TODAY

Jesus is the same today as he was yesterday, and he will be the same tomorrow (Hebrews 13:8). The Holy Spirit who filled the church on Pentecost and empowered them to give themselves fully to serving God is the same Holy Spirit who fills us today. So God can do the same thing with me and you and our churches that he has done before. I have seen what can happen today when followers of Jesus take his call seriously.

A CHURCH OF STEWARDS

In a certain village church outside Kenya's capital city, Nairobi, church leaders constantly fought over money and demanded that church members give more. But they never produced a budget or informed the members how they spent the money. Two powerful men on the board were found stealing from the offering, but no one removed them from their position.

Instead of fighting with the leadership, a group of families decided to form a new church and leave the corrupt leaders to themselves. The new group determined not to cry for outside funding, but to depend on themselves and the Lord for everything they needed. They would be transparent and accountable about how offerings would be handled. Their new pastor would be paid a living wage, so that his family would not fear poverty. In return, the pastor would avoid temptation by having nothing to do with the offering or the church accounts.

Excited to be part of what God was doing, the members eagerly gave their funds, time, and skills. They met in a local school. Then they found a piece of land and within a couple of months they raised enough money among themselves to purchase it. There the church built a temporary structure without having to hire a contractor. Everyone helped. By the time the structure was finished, the church had grown from 80 to more than 200 regular attenders.

The church leaders were open to members' ideas for new ministries. Soon the church had budgeted support for missionary work in a remote corner of the country, begun a programme helping women in the church start their own businesses, and regularly supported their denomination's seminary.

As the church raised funds to construct a large permanent place of worship, they decided to match their giving with funds to build a school for disadvantaged children in their local community. Even though it was an immense amount of money, both the leaders and the members felt God's call. They decided not to accept money from outside sources or take loans.

The congregation, now 400 members, gave generously to the weekly offering because they knew their giving was safe from corruption and was making a real difference. It took two years, but the church raised the money for both the school and the church building. What had been a field of maize became a beautiful sanctuary and a primary school for poor children.

Over a thousand people attended the first service in the new building. The community had always been branded as poor and told that they would never accomplish anything. This church filled their neighbourhood with hope by their inspiring example.

Several years later, the new sanctuary is now full every Sunday. The leadership has a new vision for a ministry centre and a hospital since healthcare is difficult to access in their area. The congregation gives toward the work with a generosity unimaginable before, even enabling them to purchase a large piece of land next to the church. This is what practising stewardship can do!

We see what we are and what we have from God's perspective.

When the Holy Spirit gets hold of us, things don't stay the same. We see ourselves from God's perspective, and we repent. We see the church from God's perspective, and we feel a new sense of calling and mission. We see what we are and what we have from God's perspective. We begin to display Christ's presence in our community. Self-centred Christians or self-centred churches hardly become people and communities that are free to be what God is calling us to be. *We* become the blessing that God wants to pour out in the lives of the lost, broken, addicted, and poor. This is not something just for leaders or for ministers. We are all called to be stewards.

God is looking for people who have fully surrendered to him. God is looking for people willing to do whatever he wants them to do and go wherever he wants them to go. He will change our hearts and shift our priorities. Through his Holy Spirit, God will transform us into stewards.

He is calling us to love. To serve. To follow him. *God wants people who become his partners.* Are we willing to live out Jesus's radical call together?

BIBLE STUDY TEN

RECLAIMING REAL STEWARDSHIP

As we finish our study, we return to the Sermon on the Mount, where Jesus clearly lays out his manifesto for discipleship, his agenda for a new way of living together in the Kingdom of God. In Matthew 5–7, he explains God's intentions underlying the Jewish law. But these ancient Jewish emphases require a heart transformation. Stewardship in Jesus's hands becomes a lens through which one's heart comes into focus. Stewardship becomes the way we fulfil the greatest commandments, how we love God with all our heart, how we love our neighbour as ourselves. Through vivid contrast and shocking statements, Jesus points out that the ways of this world neither provide the returns they promise nor bring us happy endings. But God intends something better and bigger for each human life, a return to the reason we were created. The way to regain his paradise and his reward is through his way of stewardship, walking in the footsteps of men and women from the last 2000 years who have taken Jesus seriously.

As we finish our study, we return to the Sermon on the Mount in Matthew, where Jesus clearly lays out his radical money manifesto, his agenda for a new way of living together in the Kingdom of God.

Matthew 5:1-12; 6:1-4, 19-34

5:1 When Jesus saw the crowds, he went up the mountain; and after he
sat down, his disciples came to him. 2 Then he began to speak, and
taught them, saying:

3 'Blessed are the poor in spirit, for theirs is the kingdom of heaven.

4 'Blessed are those who mourn, for they will be comforted.

5 'Blessed are the meek, for they will inherit the earth.

6 'Blessed are those who hunger and thirst for righteousness, for they will be filled.

7 'Blessed are the merciful, for they will receive mercy.

8 'Blessed are the pure in heart, for they will see God.

9 'Blessed are the peacemakers, for they will be called children of God.

10 'Blessed are those who are persecuted for righteousness' sake, for theirs is the kingdom of heaven.

11 'Blessed are you when people revile you and persecute you and
utter all kinds of evil against you falsely on my account. 12 Rejoice and
be glad, for your reward is great in heaven, for in the same way they
persecuted the prophets who were before you . . .

6:1 'Beware of practising your piety before others in order to be seen by them; for then you have no reward from your Father in heaven.

2 'So whenever you give alms, do not sound a trumpet before you, as
the hypocrites do in the synagogues and in the streets, so that they
may be praised by others. Truly I tell you, they have received their
reward. 3 But when you give alms, do not let your left hand know what
your right hand is doing, 4 so that your alms may be done in secret;
and your Father who sees in secret will reward you . . .

6:19 'Do not store up for yourselves treasures on earth, where moth and
rust consume and where thieves break in and steal; 20 but store up for
yourselves treasures in heaven, where neither moth nor rust consumes
and where thieves do not break in and steal. 21 For where your treasure
is, there your heart will be also.

22 'The eye is the lamp of the body. So, if your eye is healthy, your whole
body will be full of light; 23 but if your eye is unhealthy, your whole
body will be full of darkness. If then the light in you is darkness, how
great is the darkness!

24 'No one can serve two masters; for a slave will either hate the one
and love the other, or be devoted to the one and despise the other.
You cannot serve God and wealth.

25 'Therefore I tell you, do not worry about your life, what you will eat
or what you will drink, or about your body, what you will wear. Is not
life more than food, and the body more than clothing? 26 Look at the
birds of the air; they neither sow nor reap nor gather into barns, and
yet your heavenly Father feeds them. Are you not of more value than
they? 27 And can any of you by worrying add a single hour to your span
of life? 28 And why do you worry about clothing? Consider the lilies of
the field, how they grow; they neither toil nor spin, 29 yet I tell you,
even Solomon in all his glory was not clothed like one of these. 30 But
if God so clothes the grass of the field, which is alive today and
tomorrow is thrown into the oven, will he not much more clothe you
– you of little faith? 31 Therefore do not worry, saying, "What will we
eat?" or "What will we drink?" or "What will we wear?" 32 For it is the
Gentiles who strive for all these things; and indeed your heavenly
Father knows that you need all these things. 33 But strive first for the
kingdom of God and his righteousness, and all these things will be
given to you as well.

34 'So do not worry about tomorrow, for tomorrow will bring worries of
its own. Today's trouble is enough for today.'

Questions to Discuss

1. What emotions or feeling words do you see in the passage? How do these feelings compare to your own feelings?
2. List all the types of people and actions Jesus says will receive an inheritance or reward. What observations can you make about this list?
3. What other good things or promises does Jesus offer as he describes this new way of living?
4. To what extent do you think it is okay for Christians to be motivated by reward?
5. Which of the rewards or promises sounds the most motivating to you?

6. We need Jesus to give us new hearts and renew our minds to value what he values, so we will share his eternal inheritance. Take a few moments to reflect on what you have learned as a group, then pray together.

ABOUT THE AUTHOR

Dr Joseph William Black is a long-time missionary who has been training leaders for churches in Africa since 2000. His passion for stewardship comes from his experience serving churches in Ethiopia and Kenya, including pastoring the largest English-language church in Ethiopia. He brings a unique biblical and historical perspective on stewardship, with a BA from Duke University, an MDiv from Gordon-Conwell Theological Seminary, and a PhD in history from the University of Cambridge.

He has taught theology and history at several institutions in Africa, including the Ethiopian Graduate School of Theology in Addis Ababa and the Nairobi Evangelical Graduate School of Theology, now part of Africa International University in Nairobi. He is currently Senior Lecturer in Theology and History at St. Paul's University in Limuru, Kenya, and Senior Lecturer at Makarios III Patriarchal Orthodox Seminary in Nairobi, where he currently lives. He has previously published *Reformation Pastors: Richard Baxter and the Ideal of the Reformed Pastor* (Paternoster 2004) and many other articles on matters of history, theology, and missiology.

ACKNOWLEDGEMENTS

My life has been blessed and enriched by the input and examples of many people along the way, but two people stand out as particular examples to me of what it means to be a good steward of who they are and what they have. Father John Wangaru has been my friend here in Nairobi for more than a decade. I have watched him quietly give his time, his means, and his abilities to help the people in the parish, at the seminary, and at the monastery where he serves. I, too, have been in the circle of those so blessed. This is simply who he is, and he reminds me of Christ in so many ways. The second is Sister Photini (Megan Englebach) of St. Barbara Monastery near Santa Paula, CA. Sister Photini was a missionary at the seminary in Nairobi when I was assigned to teach here in 2015. She very graciously listened to my ponderings and complaints as I tried to get my mind around how our seminary students understood stewardship, or didn't, as the case may be. A lot of the ideas that became this book came out of our conversations. Her own commitment to Christ and her example as a good steward of all she is and all she has continues to challenge me deeply. Father John and Sister Photini, thank you for pointing me again and again to Christ. It is my prayer that this book may have the same effect on the ones who read it and take it to heart. Through the prayers of our holy fathers and mothers, Lord Jesus Christ our God, have mercy on us and save us.

ENDNOTES

1 Although I use the word *covenant*, I am not talking about covenant theology in the way covenant theologians have understood it. My views on God's covenant with Israel at Mount Sinai, Jesus's ministry in the context of that covenant, and Paul's understanding of how Christ's death and resurrection affect those outside the covenant with Israel have been influenced more by a movement known as the New Perspective on Paul. During my time at Duke, I encountered E. P. Sanders and his book *Paul and Palestinian Judaism* (Philadelphia: Fortress Press, 1977). His work was furthered by the prolific and influential New Testament scholar, N. T. Wright. For those interested in learning more, I recommend:

N. T. Wright, *Paul in Fresh Perspective* (Minneapolis: Fortress Press, 2005).

—, *Justification: God's Plan and Paul's Vision* (London: SPCK, 2009).

Those who prefer to dive deep may enjoy his three-part series: *Christian Origins and the Question of God:*

—, *The New Testament, and the People of God* (Minneapolis: Fortress Press, 1992).

—, *Jesus, and the Victory of God* (Minneapolis: Fortress Press, 1996).

—, *The Resurrection of the Son of God* (Minneapolis: Fortress Press, 2003).

—, "New Perspectives on Paul" (lecture, Edinburgh Dogmatics Conference, Edinburgh, 2003), http://ntwrightpage.com/2016/07/12/new-perspectives-on-paul/. This lecture explains how and why Wright came to his position and his response to the controversy it has generated:

2 In addition to N. T. Wright, Prof. Meredith Kline also challenged my thinking regarding the covenant and prophets in his courses "Old Testament Hermeneutics and Old Testament Prophets" at Gordon-Conwell Theological Seminary, which I took in 1987-1988.

3 My original research discovered these different aspects of the Sinai covenant "tithe". I have since discovered others who have made the same point. See, for example:

Andreas Kostenberger and David A. Croteau, " 'Will a Man Rob God?' (Malachi 3:8): A Study of Tithing in the Old and New Testaments," *Bulletin for Biblical Research* 16, no. 1 (2006): 53-77, https://www.ibr-bbr.org/files/bbr/BBR_2006a_04-Kostengerger_Croteau.pdf. Accessed 22 December 2020.

4 For an overview of the issues around how Christians should relate to the OT law, see especially section 4 of:

N. T. Wright, "The Letter to the Galatians: Exegesis and Theology," in *Between Two Horizons: Spanning New Testament Studies and Systematic Theology*, eds. Joel B. Green and Max Turner (Grand Rapids, MI: Eerdmans, 2000), 205-36, http://ntwrightpage.com/2016/07/12/the-letter-to-the-galatians-exegesis-and-theology. Accessed 22 December 2020.

5 Christians have often assumed we are obligated to keep the Ten Commandments. But in his letter to the Galatians, Paul assumes that the stipulations of the Sinai covenant could not be made obligatory for Gentiles without also forcing them to become Jews. Since the Ten Commandments are universally understood as the shorthand summary statement of the Sinai covenant, it follows that Christians are not obliged to keep them, any more than they are obliged to keep the rules regarding circumcision, eating kosher, festivals, fasts, tithing, etc. This does not mean, as some have charged, that Christians are free from the obligation to keep any law. Jesus, Paul, and James, etc., indicate that while the Old Covenant is obsolete, the New Covenant inaugurated by Jesus now defines our behaviour, morality, worship, discipleship, and stewardship as reconciled followers of the crucified and

risen Messiah living in the new age of the Kingdom of God. Jesus radically redefined the source of kingdom morality when he told the Torah expert which were the two greatest commandments (Matthew 22:37-40). Christian morality is rooted in God's revelation of himself in the Old Testament but is now based on the way set forth by Jesus and the apostles (John 14:6).

6 The longest passage about tithes in the New Testament is Melchizedek receiving a tithe from Abraham in the Old Testament (Hebrews 7:8-17), which is in the context of the Old Covenant. Jesus also mentions tithes in terms of Old Covenant obligations. He points out the hypocrisy of Pharisees who are overly concerned (for example) to give a tenth of tiny bits of herbs while ignoring the greater requirements to love one's neighbour (Matthew 23:23; Luke 11:42). In another parable, Jesus mentions a Pharisee boasting about his own righteousness in prayer to God (Luke 18:12). Jesus is not interested in changing the *Torah* requirements concerning tithing (Matthew 5:17); rather he is concerned about demonstrating the hypocrisy of those who claim to be keeping the law (*Torah*) while their lives and relationships tell a very different story. Jesus came to make a new covenant, which includes a new understanding of stewardship. That is why no subsequent writing by any apostle or Church Father takes from this mention that we must therefore all keep the Sinai covenant laws with respect to tithing.

7 Irenaeus, *Against Heresies,* IV, 18:1, 2.

8 Thanks to Sister Photini Englebach for bringing this to my attention.

9 Lev. R. 34:8. Quoted in "Charity (Tzedakah): Charity Throughout Jewish History," *The Jewish Virtual Library*, last modified 2008, https://www.jewishvirtuallibrary.org/charity-throughout-jewish-history#2.

10 See my article, "Dependency, *Harambees*, and the Struggle for Christian Stewardship in the Orthodox Churches of Kenya" in *Pharos Journal of Theology*, 98 (2017), https://www.pharosjot.com/uploads/7/1/6/3/7163688/article_17_vol_98_2017.pdf. Accessed 25 December 2020.

11 The details of Anthony's life are told by the famous fourth-century theologian and persecuted Patriarch of Alexandria, Athanasius. Read more at https://christianhistoryinstitute.org/study/module/antony. Accessed 25 December 2020.

12 This story is summarized from Emmanuel Katongole, *Born from Lament: The Theology and Politics of Hope in Africa* (Grand Rapids, MI: William B. Eerdmans Publishing, 2017), 202-219. Thanks to Hannah Rasmussen for bringing this story to my attention.

13 F. Scott Spencer, "Commentary on Acts 4:32-25," *Working Preacher*, https://www.workingpreacher.org/preaching.aspx?commentary_id=294. Accessed 26 December 2020.

14 John Holbert observes that Acts 4:32-35 in particular "has been characterized as either a rich call to a serious Christianity or the dangerous call to a life of socialism." He believes the passage should not be interpreted as a commentary on capitalism or communism. Rather, the early Christians' concern for the needy was how they bore witness to the Lord's resurrection.

John Holbert, "Holding All Things in Common: Reflections on Acts 4:32-35," *Patheos*, last modified April 8, 2012, http://www.patheos.com/Progressive-Christian/Holding-All-Things-in-Common-John-Holbert-04-09-2012. Accessed 26 December 2020.

15 Jason Jackson is worried about association with 19th- and 20th-century Marxists. Forced redistribution of wealth, he writes, "is not a biblical concept. It does not represent the facts recorded by Luke and it does not conform to the sum of God's Word pertaining to these

matters . . . [For example] Not everyone received a distribution of what was laid at the apostles' feet. 'It was distributed to each as any had need' (Acts 4:35)."

Jason Jackson, "Should Christians Have All Things in Common?" *ChristianCourier.com*, https://www.christiancourier.com/articles/1204-should-christians-have-all-things-in-common. Accessed 26 December 2020.

16 David Bentley Hart comes to a similar conclusion in his article:

David Bentley Hart, "Are Christians Supposed to Be Communists?" *The New York Times*, November 4, 2017, https://www.nytimes.com/2017/11/04/opinion/sunday/christianity-communism.html. Accessed 26 December 2020.

17 John Holbert agrees. "Holding All Things in Common. Reflections on Acts 4:32-35," http://www.patheos.com/Progressive-Christian/Holding-All-Things-in-Common-John-Holbert-04-09-2012. Accessed 26 December 2020.

18 The word *deacon* is not used in Acts 6:1-7 to describe the ministry of the men who are chosen to help the apostles "wait on tables". Church tradition, however, identifies these men as the first members of the diaconate.

19 Rodney Stark, *The Rise of Christianity: How the Obscure, Marginal Jesus Movement Became the Dominant Religious Force in the Western World in a Few Centuries* (Princeton, NJ: Princeton University Press, 1996), 161-162.

20 Irenaeus, *Against Heresies*, IV, 18:1, 2; emphasis added.

21 The following quotations from the *Didache* are found at https://www.ccel.org/ccel/richardson/fathers.viii.i.iii.html. Accessed 27 December 2020.

22 Hadrian, quoted by John Ferguson in *Clement of Alexandria* (New York, NY: Twayne Publishers, 1974), 20.

23 Clement of Alexandria, *Who Is the Rich Man That Shall Be Saved?* William Wilson, tr., in Alexander Roberts and James Donaldson, eds., *Ante-Nicene Fathers*, 2 (Peabody, MA: Hendrickson Publishers, [1885] 1994), 595.

24 Clement of Alexandria, *Who Is the Rich Man That Shall Be Saved?*, 595-596.

25 Of Minucius Felix almost nothing is known. The date of his death is an estimate. He certainly predates Cyprian and may be a contemporary of Tertullian. All that survives of him is this one work, an apologetic dialogue between a Christian and a pagan.

26 G. W. Clarke, tr., *The Octavius of Marcus Minucius Felix* (New York, NY: Newman Press, 1974), 119.

27 Cyprian, *On the Lapsed,* 6. In A. Cleveland Coxe, Alexander Roberts, and Sir James Donaldson, *Ante-Nicene Fathers*, 5 (Peabody, MA: Hendrickson Publishers 1994 [1886]), 438.

28 Paraphrase by Charles White, "Clement of Alexandria: What Kind of Rich Person Can Be Saved?" in *Christian History* 6, no. 2. (1987), https://www.christianitytoday.com/history/issues/issue-14/clement-of-alexandria-what-kind-of-rich-person-can-be-saved. Accessed 17 January 2021.

29 Ibid.

30 M. F. Toal, *The Sunday Sermons of the Great Fathers*, 3 (NP: CreateSpace Independent Publishing Platform, 2011), 331.

31 Ibid.

32 Ibid, 332.

33 See M. R. P. McGuire, 'De Nabuthae,' in *Patristic Studies,* 15 (Washington, D.C.: The Catholic University of America, 1927), 46-103l; see also Migne, PL, 14, 765-792, http://hymnsandchants.com/Texts/Sermons/Ambrose/OnNaboth.htm. Accessed 26 December 2020.

34 Ibid.

35 Augustine, *Expositions of the Psalms* 121-150, Maria Boulding, tr. (New York, NY: New City Press, 2004), 159-160.

36 John Chrysostom, *On Wealth and Poverty* (Crestwood, NY: St. Vladimir's Seminary Press, 1984), 49.

37 Ibid.

38 Ibid., 50.

39 Robert Holet reminds us: "The [Greek] term *oikonomos* (steward, house manager) . . . appears frequently in the New Testament, particularly in parables where Jesus describes the 'servant' (disciple) as an *oikonomos*. [The Eastern churches see its natural meaning as applied first to the church.] Orthodoxy also relates the term of *oikonomia* (stewardship) to that of *episkopos* – overseer, bishop, who is responsible for the oversight of the household of God (Acts 20:28, Titus 1:7, 1 Timothy 3) . . . [For the early Christians and] in Orthodoxy, the term *oikonomia* was never seen as strictly a matter of pragmatic management of personal or corporate financial affairs, but rather referred more broadly to the whole of human life and the manner in which Christian life is to be lived, the spiritual dimension being preeminent. As each Christian is to be a responsible steward, the bishop has the vocation to be chief steward of the local church. There was no sense of a separate 'theology of stewardship' in Orthodoxy, any more than there was a 'theology of ethic' or a 'theology of spirituality', rather Orthodoxy always focused on the multidimensional aspects of Christian life as a whole, of which what we call stewardship was an integral part." Culturally, the many different ethnic groups across the continent are much more holistic in their approach to life than their Western counterparts, so the early churches' holistic Christianity would likely resonate with most African Christians, if they knew such a thing existed!

Robert Holet, *The First and the Finest: Orthodox Christian Stewardship as Sacred Offering* (Bloomington, IN: Author House, 2013), 39-40.

40 Klaus Bockmühl, "On Wealth and Stewardship," *Christianity Today*, June 23, 1978, https://www.christianitytoday.com/ct/1978/june-23/current-religious-thought-on-wealth-and-stewardship.html.

41 M. F. Toal, *The Sunday Sermons of the Great Fathers*, 3 (NP: CreateSpace Independent Publishing Platform, 2011), 332.

RAISING UP GOOD STEWARDS

Joseph William Black

For anyone who leads a church, an organization, or a ministry in Africa, *Raising Up Good Stewards* expands upon the concepts of *The Radical Money Manifesto* with practical solutions for ministry.

Find out how to:

- Increase church giving with integrity
- Support your family and the needy
- Restore the church's witness and credibility in corrupt contexts

Solving the money problems in your church doesn't require outside donors or unethical shortcuts. Learn from God's people – in the Bible, church history, and in today's churches in Africa. As we become good stewards using what Jesus has entrusted to us, he will use us to bless our world.

Order from oasisinternationalpublishing.com

OASIS INTERNATIONAL

Satisfying Africa's Thirst for God's Word

Our mission is to grow discipleship through publishing African voices.
Go to oasisinternationalpublishing.com to learn more.

INFLUENCE: LEADING WITHOUT POSITION
Philip E. Morrison & Hankuri Tawus Gaya
Do you have ideas for how to change your community, church, or nation – but feel powerless to make them happen? This book tells you how you can influence others to take action and start change, just as young men and women in the Bible did.

HIGHLY FAVOURED: OUR POWERFUL GOD'S COVENANT WITH YOU
Stuart J. Foster
The God of the Bible is not unreliable or inaccessible like the spiritual beings in African traditional religions. He chooses to have a covenant relationship with his people and we do not have to earn God's favour.

AFRICANS AND AFRICA IN THE BIBLE
Tim Welch
This book shows the presence and the participation of Africans in the biblical text, helping demonstrate that Christianity is not a "white man's religion" and that Christianity has deep roots in African soil.

AFRICAN CHRISTIAN THEOLOGY REVISITED
Richard J. Gehman
For all African Christians, *African Christian Theology Revisited* is a powerful plea to think through your faith in African contexts under the authority of the Word of God.

HELPING WITHOUT HURTING IN AFRICA
Jonny Kabiswa Kyazze and Anthony Sytsma with Brian Fikkert
This book trains leaders to proclaim the gospel in both word and deed, changing mind-sets and helping them apply biblical principles to care wisely and compassionately for people who are poor without unintentionally doing harm.

LEARNING TO LEAD
Richard J. Gehman
With its discussion questions and practical applications, this book will guide you to obtaining character and skills and help you become an effective Christian leader. It was written from the living experience of African leaders and it has been shaped by 36 years of training church leaders in Kenya.

ANSWERS FOR YOUR MARRIAGE
Bruce and Carol Britten
Offers practical insights to marriage issues and facts on sex, pregnancy, family planning, child-raising, money issues, adultery, HIV, and sex-related diseases. If your marriage is in despair, look to this book for some answers for your marriage.

PARENTING WITH PURPOSE & AFRICAN WISDOM
Gladys K. Mwiti
This practical guide for Christians is a relevant, thoughtful presentation on the characteristics of parenting that delivers results.

OASIS INTERNATIONAL PUBLISHING

oasisinternationalpublishing.com | oasisinternational.com